The Contented Retirement

Leisure activities
that keep the mind lively

Stephen McAdam

Published by

MELROSE BOOKS

An Imprint of Melrose Press Limited
St Thomas Place, Ely
Cambridgeshire
CB7 4GG, UK
www.melrosebooks.com

FIRST EDITION

Cover designed by Amanda Barrett Creative Design

ISBN 1 905226 76 4

Printed and bound in Great Britain by:
CPI Antony Rowe, Bumpers Farm,
Chippenham, Wiltshire, SN14 6LH, UK

Dedication

To my dearest Danièle and Johanna

Acknowledgements

My especial thanks are due to Garry Thorne, who spurred me to ideas for content, and edited and motivated my faltering efforts in the early days; Douglas and Beryl Dow who constructively reviewed many of the chapters as the book moved forward; and Harry Seydoux and John Miles, each providing invaluable input.

Contents

CHAPTER 1

Tracing Your Roots

AN INTRODUCTION TO GENEALOGY

Have you ever thought about making an in-depth study of your family roots, to find out who your ancestors were and how far back they can be traced?

Were they perhaps writers or scholars in the 19th century, a fascinating period of European history? If one of your ancestors was a famous industrialist or military hero, this knowledge has possibly been handed down from parent to child over the ages. Certainly, if your family name is a Watt, Bell, Edison, Ford or a Fleming, it could mean that your roots include links to a pioneer of one of the core elements of today's world. Or, more likely, did your forebears play out their working lives anonymously in the iron and coal industries, which fuelled the 18th century Industrial Revolution, or on the land, tilling the soil or raising livestock?

If none of your ancestors are known at present to have been persons of outstanding achievement, you may still be interested to know more about them: where they were born; where they spent their lives; what they did for a living. National and cultural roots can have a genetic influence on your own or your children's or grandchildren's characters. Funny things genes, they can disappear and pop up centuries later. You might also be interested to learn about some of the history of the times when they were alive, their lifestyles and how they survived the constantly recurring wars around Europe.

Or you might just want to try to track down members of your family or friends that you have lost trace of over the years.

BRINGING FAMILY MEMBERS TOGETHER

The affinity of family members varies considerably from one family to another. Also, geography plays a part in family ties. For instance, northern European families members are typically less united than those in southern Europe, for example in Spain and Italy, where family ties are strong and reunions frequent, rather like in that film with Marlon Brando as The Godfather.

If you were to decide to take up genealogy as a pastime, your research would probably of necessity include contact with other family members who have been living remotely from the main family base for many years and thus have lost contact. As they say, out of sight is out of mind. Your research could have a knock-on effect in bringing family members closer together than they have been in the past due to a lack of common interest in family affairs. You might just find another family member who has also embarked on researching their ancestral roots and can pool information with you.

The discovery of a high achiever such as a valour decorated military ancestor, successful researcher or such like, can work wonders for family esteem.

MOTIVATING FAMILY AMBITIONS

The identifying of distinguished and hitherto unknown lifetime occupations of ancestors such as service to country, local community or humanity, sporting achievements or professions, can motivate the youngest generation family members to follow in their footsteps, thus shaping their studies and careers.

HOW TO GO ABOUT IT

Tools required

Access to the internet can help enormously. Throughout this book, you will find references to websites to search for information. If you are not already skilled in personal computers, it is quite possible that some of the younger members of your family or friends have those skills and can help out. It is estimated that nowadays around 100 million Europeans use the internet. Also chapter 5, Surfing the Web, is an introduction as to how personal computing and the internet is nowadays a wonderful means to access intelligence.

Search engines such as Google and Yahoo have masses of information tentacles, not only to help track down people but also to provide links to websites of organizations holding public records of births, marriages, deaths, cemeteries, military service and population census records dating back to the 19th century.

If you do not have access to a computer, however, do not be deterred. An inquisitive mind and tenacity is all that is required to trace your family origins, using public archives, old family papers and photos and enquiries within the family network.

Family names

Genealogy is all about generations of people bearing the same family name. In most of the western world normally the father's surname is the one which is passed on to offspring. One notable exception to this general rule is in Spain where children are legally registered with two surnames, the first their father's and the other that of their mother. Thus, in a name like José Luis Rodriguez Zapatero, his father was a Senor Rodriguez and his mother a Senorita Zapatero. This Spanish custom probably arises out of respect to the lady of the family who, after all, does the hard work when it comes to bringing children into the world and rearing them.

Some modern generation young ladies, especially those following a career, hold on to their surname when they get married and tag on their new husband's surname as a second family surname, like that well-known former First Lady, Hilary Rodham Clinton. Indeed, this is a follow-on to the old English custom of what was referred to as double-barrelled names, when often the new bride, with a hitch of her skirts and the stamp of a pretty foot, firmly refused to drop her daddy's family name and placed it in front of her husband's surname; especially if her new husband's name was a Smith or a Jones and her daddy's name was a Churchill or a Gladstone.

As society becomes more liberal, new laws, such as in France, may give the mother the option of having her child legally registered with her own surname and not the father's. Such a practice will put the proverbial cat amongst the pigeons for future genealogists trying to trace ancestral roots.

Given names

One very interesting aspect of tracing one's roots is discovering the first names given to your forebears over generations and perhaps handed down, out of family pride, to sons and daughters. Families where popular first names such as James and John, and Mary and Jean, run from generation to generation, especially combined with surnames such as Smith and Jones, can seize on a more distinctive first name found in the genealogical search, say, a Gregory or a Johanna, to break with tradition and bestow their son or daughter with alternative first names which still stem from the family roots.

Family tree

Historically, the Family Tree, the sketch of "who procreated who" in families has always had one great drawback.

The family tree is a male preserve, a real male chauvinistic pig! All those cuddly little girls born into a family are included in the tree, but, when they grow up and get married, they float like a leaf to the ground in autumn. And, of course, join another family tree for a one note entry and then it is back to the male's surname for descendents. Effectively it can be said that, in family trees, boys are the branches and girls autumn leaves.

Start with what is already known

The first step is to locate your family stock of birth, marriage and death (BMDs) certificates. BMDs have been in existence in Britain since 1837 and, since they are legal, are documents that are normally put away in a safe place and safeguarded when moving house.

Also personal diaries, letters, newspaper cuttings, obituaries, property deeds, wills, passports and driving licenses are part of the genealogical treasure trove with potential to yield a host of interesting stuff about the family, their lives and friends; enough to make the bloodhound in you start wagging its tail and sniffing for further clues.

Also all those old family photos that may have been gathering dust in the attic for years are a great source of information. How far back in time can one expect photos of ancestors? The answer to that is mid-19th century since the very first photos appeared in the 1840s after William Fox Talbot developed the art of printing photos on paper from negatives in 1839. Snapshots of family and friends did not become widespread until the turn of the 20th century after George Eastman, the inventor of roll film in 1881, founded Eastman Kodak in the US to produce the Brownie box camera for sale to the general public.

These old photos are often stored away and forgotten, some of these great photos in sepia of grandfathers and grandmothers, well dressed and dignified, posing with their children in front of an old box camera in the early 1900s. Pictures like those are a great medium to arouse family values and solidarity and raise questions about who those appearing in the photos were and what became of them. Old group wedding photos are especially useful since they contain many close family members.

If you have a computer, put those old pictures through a scanner and load them into your PC. Now they are ready to send off to other family members, to jog memories in putting the ancestral framework together. Questions like: that delightful little girl with pigtails and a shy smile, sitting cross-legged in the front row, who was she and could she still be alive? Someone, somewhere in the family, might well know.

DRAWING UP THE FAMILY TREE

In the centre of the largest sheet of paper you can find, draw a horizontal row of small boxes. Each box should contain a family member, if married, with spouse, with their date of birth (dob) and, if applicable, date of decease (dod).

Start with your generation, that is, you and your spouse, and your sisters and brothers and their spouses. Note that this only contains information pertaining to one family name, your own.

Then add a horizontal row of boxes above your generation boxes and slot in details of the children of each couple of your generation, with a third upper row for the children from each marriage. These are the newly sprouted top branches of the family tree, rather like stars on a Christmas tree, which, of course, is exactly what they are.

Now, going towards the bottom of the tree, insert a row of boxes for the names of your parents and the names of your father's brothers and sisters and their children. Then, progressively, further below, your paternal grandparents and their relatives and so on... right down to your very roots!

If you are skilled with a computer, you can also set up and fill in your family tree boxes using one of the many software products available on the web. One such software can be found by logging on to www. familytreemaker.com.

Whatever way you choose to put the family tree together, there will be a point where you start to run out of intelligence and find lots of boxes with blanks in them. Now the real hunt starts in earnest.

Filling in the blanks

At this point, you have to scratch your head to see if you have exhausted all family sources of intelligence. Ah, yes, your cousin Julia. What, she must be now in her early eighties. She ran off and married a dashing young lieutenant in the French army after the war and was last known to be living in Toulouse. She might be able to help to find out more about your great grandparents. Is she still alive? Try to track her down via international telephone directory enquiries or the *Toulouse Mairie* (City Hall). Imagine you do find her eventually and her joy on receiving a letter or telephone call from you, eager to have news of other family members.

If you use the likes of the Family Tree Maker mentioned above, this website will conduct searches for the blanks by switching you on to another website called www. ancestry.com.

Family Tree Maker will also enable you to prepare charts and reports with any photos that you have available, which you can then click on, or mail to other family members to get them to join in the search. Tally-ho, the hunt is on!

Narrowing your research targets

Once all family sources of intelligence are fully exploited, have a good look at the family tree and select the blanks which, if identified, might provide other leads to extend your research, especially the persons who may be the most intriguing ancestors, one who might have given your name notoriety. As in my case, John Loudon McAdam (1756–1836), the Scotsman who pioneered road-making in the early 19th century. I know of a large French road construction company that has named one of its meeting rooms after my namesake, one of the roots of their industry. But we have still more digging to do if we are ever to establish links with the great man.

SEARCHING THE PUBLIC ARCHIVES

The keeping of public records of citizens in Europe started as far back as the 16th century, representing mind-boggling masses of paperwork and huge archives. With experience, you will establish the archives that can provide answers to your searches: where they are based and which helpful custodians can point you in the right direction for other sources of information. Below are some of the main ports of call to track down the missing pieces in your puzzle. Note also that the archives which appear below also have websites to consult in the first instance to mitigate travel. Did you know that research for genealogy figures in the top five motives for surfing the web?

Births, marriages and death records

For the UK, the place to start is The Family Records Centre (FRC) in Islington for traces of ancestors born in England after 1837 and, for other countries in the UK, the New Register House in Edinburgh (records commence in the 16th century – see below) and the Registrar General in Belfast. For the Irish Republic, you have the Registrar General in Dublin. For online searches you can log on to www.familyrecords.gov.uk. This website will lead you to other archives for searches around the UK.

As a starter to tracing your roots and compiling a family tree, the FRC in Islington has an ongoing programme of presentations for beginners given by experts in genealogy.

These talks take place at the FRC offices every Tuesday afternoon and Saturday morning throughout the year and might cover topics such as what the FRC offers by way of records; how to get the most out of census records online (see below); websites to select when tracing your family history via the internet; introduction to local and family history societies and so on.

From mid-16th century till the 1837 legislation, births, marriages and deaths were recorded by the village or town church where the event took place, now referred to as parish registers. Try contacting county archivists and local church records, which are also partially available in some of the national archives, such as the FRC for England and the General Register Office for Scotland (GROS), (see below) for Scotland.

Tracing the deceased in cemeteries
One approach to tracing ancestors is a visit to cemeteries
in the area where you suspect they may have lived at
the end of their lives. This can be a pleasant initiative if
one considers the dignified beauty of a well-kept village
cemetery, with all those touching tributes inscribed on
tombstones by grieving loved ones.

Population census records
A population census commenced in Britain as far back
as 1841 and has occurred every ten years since that date,
with the exception of 1941 when the Nazi onslaught
focused attention on more important matters and anyway
a large portion of the population was away in far-off
places.

For each census, from 1841 onwards, every house was
visited and the names of all occupants recorded, including
servants, lodgers and any visitors staying at the house at
the time of the census, their age, occupation, place of
birth and whether a person was blind, deaf, dumb or
insane. One has to suspect that any person, perhaps even
youngsters, who refused to talk to the census takers may
have been recorded as either dumb or insane!

The population census records for England and Wales
are available on microfilm covering 1841 onwards at the
FRC in Islington. The records of the population census
in 1901 in England and Wales are also now available
online at www.census.pro.gov.uk and involve 32 million
people.

This website for the 1901 census was made public in
2001 after being hidden away under the one hundred
year rule which prohibits disclosure. The 100-year cover-
up to preserve confidentiality under UK law is now being
challenged with a plea to reduce this to 70 to 80 years
in the light of the increasing public interest in tracing

family roots.

An example: searching in Scotland

Supposing your genealogy involves principally relatives born or living at one time in, say, Scotland which spawned so many of its people to far flung parts of the globe?

Start with contacts to the BMD records of the villages or towns in Scotland where your target ancestor is likely to have lived at some point in time. If that fails, the place to visit would be the GROS at the New Register House in Edinburgh, a vast hoard of genealogical intelligence, covering records on Scots from 1553–1854 in old parish records, BMDs from 1855 onwards, census records from 1841–1901 and much more. With a visit to national bodies such as the GROS, you would gain a wealth of insight into the techniques of genealogy research at the same time as a search for entries in your own family tree.

If you can go online, the website www.scotlandspeople. gov.uk also provides data sourced from BMD registrations from the 16th century onwards and population census records for Scotland from 1871 to 1901. At time of writing, work is proceeding in transferring old parish register data from file to computer, reducing what were usually immaculate handwritten records to digits: that's modernisation. Still, you have to admit, it makes retrieval easier.

Suggested reading:

Tracing your Scottish Ancestors: A Guide to Ancestry Research in the Scottish Record Office
by Cecil J Sinclair

For immigrants to the New World...

Alternatively, did your ancestors perhaps emigrate from Scotland or other parts of Britain to North America? One of the interesting aspects of genealogy is learning something of the history during the period in time your ancestors were alive. Here are only a few of the factors which motivated millions of young men and women to immigrate to the New World in the 19th century.

One of the most important incentives for young men in their prime to leave their countries of origin was to avoid being conscripted into military service for the almost constant wars being waged, with huge casualties and loss of life, around Europe during the 1800s.

Another factor was the potato famine in 1845–49 throughout Europe, caused by a blight which destroyed the potato crops. This blight was especially disastrous in Ireland where it almost instantly eliminated the primary food source of most of the population. The effect in Ireland was devastating, resulting in up to half a million deaths and widespread hunger and extreme hardship. Millions of people left Ireland and other parts of Europe, many bound for the US and Canada, to seek a better life. It is estimated that there are now around 44 million Irish Americans, living mainly in New York, Boston and Chicago and second only to the Germans as an ethnic group in the US.

There was also the attraction of the Homestead Act, passed by the US Congress in 1862. This act of law offered land ownership to immigrants, many of whom had been poor farm workers living under feudal conditions on estates owned by landed gentry and nobility in their countries of origin. The Homestead Act offered to each family 160 acres of land at low prices in return for a guarantee to cultivate as farmland for crops or grazing and stay for a minimum of five years.

What are the best sources to use to trace ancestors thought to have settled in the US? If you have some idea of the locality where they had settled, you can contact or visit the area's Register of Deeds office at the County

Court House where records of BMDs are held. You can also consult the United States Census records.

Censuses in the US commenced in 1790, and have been carried out every ten years ever since. The US census records remain restricted to public access for 72 years (as opposed to 100 years in the UK) and are therefore currently open to public research for the years 1790 to 1930. These records are held in The National Archives in Washington D C and its thirteen regional offices. For more information, you can consult two websites, www.nara.gov and www.census.gov.

Another good source to trace your forebears is the archives of immigrants passing through the port of New York, the prime port for ships arriving from Europe. During the years 1855–1892 passengers on ships arriving from Europe passed through Castle Gardens, the immigration station and located in lower Manhattan.

During that period, 8.2 million immigrants were received through Castle Gardens and their names, and likely destination in the US (if they knew it), were duly recorded. These records are now available at The National Archives, mentioned above.

Ellis Island, which stands alongside the island on which the Statue of Liberty was built, took over as immigration station for the port of New York in 1892 until 1924 when the US Immigration Act transferred responsibility for granting incoming visas to US consulates abroad. To research possible arrivals during the years 1892 to 1924, you can log on to www.ellisisland.org/genealogy and key in the names of your ancestors with approximate dates of arrival.

Canada was also a prime haven for many immigrants from Europe during the mass exodus from the 19th century onwards. For anyone intent on researching BMDs in Canada to fill in spaces in their family tree, the first step should be contact with the Canadian Genealogy Centre in Ottawa. You could request a free copy of their publication, Tracing Your Ancestors in Canada.

If you have access to the internet, you could also start with logging on to www.collectionscanada.ca/genealogy which gives a large choice of sources for genealogical research, including national censuses taken in 1901 and 1911 and immigrants arriving at Grosse-Ile between 1832 and 1937.

Let the Mormons help you trace your roots
A great source for people of all nationalities who wish to conduct a genealogic search via the internet is a truly superb website, www.familysearch.org, maintained by the Mormons, that is, the Church of Jesus Christ Latter-day Saints, or LDS, based in Salt Lake City in Utah.

The LDS was founded in 1894 and maintains and continually updates genealogical records of people from all over the world in a vast data bank in Salt Lake City. More than 600 million names, listed under what they call the IGI – International Genealogical Index – are held on the LDS computers and can be accessed via the internet. There is a possibility that your name might just be on computer.

If you open the familysearch.org site and click on "the Church", then "Families", you will see that the Mormon church has the sacred belief that family relationships are meant to last forever. Hence, the maintenance of genealogical records of persons, living and deceased and from many countries, for access to all. There is no need for anyone to join the Mormon Church in order to benefit from the search facilities and access is free, except for special requests for information.

Here is only one illustration, taken from countless options, of what you can achieve by logging on to familysearch.org. Say, you seek to trace an ancestor, a one George Wilson and your research to date indicates that he probably was born around 1880, place not known, but in England. On the website, click on to "Search for Ancestors" and then fill in the name, estimated dob and indicate "England" (you have a choice of countries ranging from Afghanistan to Zimbabwe on the site).

Then click on "search" and you will have a whole list of George Wilsons from which to select. Ah, here's one, born in Chatham, Kent, could he be our ancestor? Click on his name and you will then get the name of his father, father's occupation, address and so on.

Searching through a site like familysearch.org is kind of like wandering through a labyrinth of corridors, seeking and finding leads as to the where the next step might take you.

Researching military records
Your search might also include military records. After all, Europe has been through major conflicts during the last two centuries, with the two World Wars in the 20th century, and the Napoleonic Wars in 1792–1815 when France, under Napoleon, ran amok and campaigned against Britain, Prussia, Austria, Portugal and Russia. There was also the Crimean War in 1854–56, with the Russians pitted against the British, French and Turks, with a monumental casualty list. The Public Records Office in Kew, London maintains military records dating back to 1861, some even as far back as 1761.

Many, many persons died in all these monstrous conflicts, particularly the 1914–18 war with huge death toll in war zones like Flanders. For ancestors whom you suspect might have perished in both the 1914–18 and World War II, check also with the Commonwealth War Graves Commission based in Maidenhead. Their website, www.cwgc.org, is a mine of information, including where the victims of war are buried. This could well present an opportunity to travel there and pay homage. The CWGC website also gives names of parents and spouses which, in itself, could advance the preparation of the family tree.

So, let us leave the killing fields of Normandy and Flanders with their green and white, well kept graveyards, row on row of testimonies to the ultimate sacrifice for king and country. And return to reflect on what you can gain from tracing your roots.

As indicated above, genealogy can provide an engrossing pastime which can generate pleasure and stimulation in achieving results, whilst demanding an intellectual effort, guile and tenacity against the odds of the unknown.

On the material side, tracing your roots can give opportunity for travel with a purpose and meeting new people, including possibly members of your own family that you never knew existed.

... AND DON'T FORGET, NOBODY'S PERFECT!

As a final note, we must also learn to accept the odd setback, such as the ancestor, unearthed from the genealogical labyrinth, who might not come up to one's own standards. The National Archives in Kew has some records of convicts transported from Britain to its colonies during the 18th century.

In those days, the British judicial system adopted an alternative to hanging some convicted criminals: that of shipping them to overseas colonies, where they were interned. The first batches were transported to America but the outbreak of the American Revolution in 1776 put paid to that destination as a haven from the gallows and Australia was chosen as the alternative.

In May 1787, the first fleet of five transport ships, accompanied by two warships, set sail from Britain, bound for Australia with 717 convicts on board, in such deplorable conditions that, eight months later, when the fleet arrived in Port Jackson, Australia, 48 of them had died en route. Internment of these early settlers was in a penal colony in Sydney. During the following 80 years, a total of 160,000 convicts were shipped to Australia, many of them later freed, to be counted as part of the continent's first settlers; they and their descendents now meriting a slot in somebody's family tree.

So, when tracing your roots, always bear in mind the closing line to that great 1959 film, Some Like It Hot, when Jack Lemmon, masquerading as a woman, admitted he was a man, Joe E Brown quipped, "Well, nobody's perfect". Most families have a black sheep hidden somewhere, sometime in the murky past.

For those of you who may have ancestors who joined the flood of people of all nationalities from Europe and other parts of the world to Australia to seek a new life during the 19th and 20th centuries, The National Library of Australia has massive archives covering immigration, passenger lists, BMDs, cemeteries, military service and much more, even records of these first settler convicts. For starters, you could log on to www.nla.gov.au./oz/genelist.

Suggested reading to have a more detailed guide to tracing your roots:

Who Do You Think You Are?
    by Dan Waddell, published by BBC books.
Family History Starter Pack
    by Simon Fowler, published by National Archives.
Ancestral Trails, the Complete Guide to British Genealogy and Family
    by Mark Herber.

CHAPTER 2

Anyone For Bridge?

AN INSIGHT INTO A GREAT CARD GAME

You have certainly heard many people talk enthusiastically about bridge, they maybe even want you to join them as a bridge partner or become a member of their club.

This chapter will first look at the origins of bridge and some of the great players who made the game what it is today, and then provide a basic outline of how bridge is played and what the game has to offer as a pastime for retirement. The chapter will also present suggestions to beginners as to what has to be done to take up the game.

IN THE BEGINNING

The history of bridge dates back to the 17th century when the game began life as whist, with four players, split into two teams playing against each other. Whist was much in vogue with the English nobility. The first book devoted to whist, Edmund Hoyle's Short Treatise, appeared in 1742 and became a bestseller. The game's popularity quickly spread, notably to Turkey and other parts of the Middle East and around Europe.

In 1886, Tolstoy wrote in his novel The Death of Ivan Ilyich, "The pleasures Ivan Ilyich derived from his work were those of pride; the pleasures he derived from society were those of vanity; but it was genuine pleasure that he derived from whist".

During the 19th century, duplicate whist was conceived whereby, in competition whist, the same hands derived from the first deal of cards were played several times over by successive players. This was to eliminate the element of luck of the deal and to award credit for skilled play. The first game of duplicate reportedly took place in London in 1857. Today's duplicate bridge is played using the same principles.

In France, in the early 1900s, whist was termed *plafond* (the French word for "ceiling"). Plafond required that each team state the number of tricks they intended to take.

Popular theory also has it that the concept of dummy whist, that is, when whist is played by only three players, with the fourth hand face up on the table, was conceived by the British in the heydays of colonial India. Modern contract bridge also involves a face-up dummy hand.

WHY THE GAME IS CALLED BRIDGE

No one seems to know precisely from where the word bridge originated. One theory is that it is derived from a word in either Serbo-Croatian or Ukrainian and was imported to the game around 1860 when it was played by the diplomatic community at the Cercle d'Orient in Istanbul. An exotic and sort of Eric Ambler pedigree. Much more likely, the word comes from Russian whist, called "biritch", meaning "announcer". Bridge players announce their contract bids.

SOME GREAT BRIDGE PLAYERS

The father of contract bridge

In 1926, Harold "Mike" Vanderbilt, an American multimillionaire and three-time winner of the America's Cup, added an historic new dimension to bridge. His great grandfather was Cornelius Vanderbilt, the founder of America's railroads and his mother was a First Lady in New York High Society and the Vanderbilt family lived in a world of luxury and excess. Mike Vanderbilt was also an inveterate bridge player.

Whilst playing bridge at his yacht club, Vanderbilt and his friends developed the concept that, as a refinement of the *plafond* principle, each partnership should commit itself to taking a certain number of tricks in a "contract", that only tricks bid and achieved should count for winning and that extra tricks taken in excess of the contract be rewarded with bonuses. The term vulnerable was also devised to describe a team which is subject to higher penalties for having already won a game.

OTHERS IN THE WHO'S WHO OF BRIDGE

Many personalities, other than Vanderbilt, are worthy of note during the passage of history of bridge. Here are a few.

From the US

Ely Culbertson of the United States was one such personality who, through his consummate skills and natural flair for publicity, contributed enormously to making the game so popular, especially in the US in the 1930s.

Culbertson, an immigrant from Russia, was responsible for the first widely accredited system of bidding. He also captained the US team in highly publicized matches against British teams in 1930, 1933 and 1934 when the Americans triumphed. As inevitably happens when the press headlines such winning events, Culbertson became a national hero.

In 1931, Culbertson challenged a fellow American bridge ace, Sydney Lenz to a 150-rubber team match, maintaining that the Culbertson bidding system would prevail. This duel between two titans of the game, each with a partner, did much to spark the US public interest in bridge and, by the time Culbertson was declared the winner, bridge was becoming a popular pastime coast-to-coast.

Culbertson's reputation in the world of bridge was thus at its pinnacle in the 1930s and his Contract Bridge Blue Book became a landmark textbook of the game. He also founded the magazine, The Bridge World, still going strong to this day.

Charles Goren, another redoubtable player and author of many textbooks on bridge, gave up practicing law in the 1930s to spend his life in the world of bridge. Goren was the US national champion over 30 times and, in the late 1950s was dubbed "The King of Aces" by Time Magazine. He had published a number of books and is considered as an authority on the game.

Amongst many world leaders who embraced bridge as a worthy pastime, I should mention President Eisenhower who played regularly with top experts during his relaxation from high office in the White House.

A legendary figure from Italy

Benito Garozzo of Italy is one of many names which stand out in the annals of world bridge. Garozzo was the star member of the famous Italian "Blue Team" which dominated world bridge tournaments in the 1960s. Teams from around the globe compete annually for the Bermuda Bowl. Up till the end of the 1950s, the US had dominated the world bridge scene. The Blue Team won the Bermuda Bowl seven years in a row, from 1961 to 1967 and later in 1975 and 1976.

A great and controversial champion from Britain

Boris Shapiro was born in Latvia in 1909 but emigrated with his wealthy parents to Britain during the Russian Revolution and settled in Doncaster. A year later, at the age of ten, he was already playing cards for money. Much later, in his forties, with his love for gambling still intact, Shapiro took on the role of banker of a baccarat syndicate at Crockfords, the London gaming club.

His real love however was bridge. He won his first world bridge title with his partner, Oswald Jacoby, the World Pairs in 1932, and from then on never looked back. Shapiro was a regular member of the British team, taking the European Team Championship four times from 1948. With Terence Reese as his partner, he won Britain's sole World Open Team championship title in 1955.

In 1965, Shapiro and Reese hit the world headlines when they were accused of cheating in the World Bridge Championship held in Buenos Aires. They were charged with illegally using signals to transmit information by varying the number of fingers shown whilst holding their cards. The WBF, the World Bridge Federation, conducted an on-site hearing and found the pair guilty but passed the responsibility to the British Bridge League for a definitive verdict. During an enquiry lasting over a year, two eminent members of the British legal profession returned a verdict of not proven.

Whatever the verdict, the incident led to the introduction of bidding screens in top championships so that players cannot see each other and use body language to aid interpretation of their bids.

Shapiro continued to play world tournament bridge

with great merit and after a distinguished winning career, won the 1998 World Senior Pairs trophy, incredibly at the age of 89, with Irving Gordon as his partner. He also won Britain's most prestigious event, the Gold Cup, a record eleven times, the last in 1998, his vintage year, it seems. Boris Shapiro was author of two books and bridge columnist for the London Sunday Times.

Celebrity actor and bridge champion

The well known star of the screen of yesteryear, Omar Sharif, who starred in many films over the last 40 years, such as Dr Zhivago and who, no dummy, gained a university degree in maths and physics in his youth, has been one of the world's top bridge players most of his life. Indeed, it seems that Sharif has been a top bridge player who starred in movies from time to time, rather than the opposite. He has written a number of books on bridge. Here are a couple of his titles: Life in Bridge and Play More Bridge.

WHAT BRIDGE HAS TO OFFER

If you, like most retired persons, would like to be pleasantly occupied and meet new friends of similar tastes and interests, bridge is your passport to people of all nationalities and places because the game is universal.

Bridge is also a pastime which you can share as a couple. An example: suppose you find yourselves in an hotel somewhere delightful like the Costa Brava, towards the end of the afternoon after a day's golf or by the beach and there are a two or three of hours before dinner is served, the chances are that you will find another couple who will welcome joining you for a rubber of bridge.

Age is no real barrier as long as your mind and memory are still functioning reasonably well. Bear in mind that Boris Shapiro, albeit obviously a man of above average intelligence, won a world title at the age of 89.

Even with a beginner's level of competence, you will usually be able to play bridge amongst friends or in a club in your home area. Careful, however, even friendly bridge sessions can be regarded by many as serious stuff, so do not take it lightly. And, let's face it, there are worst ways to spend a rainy afternoon with friends, accompanied by light refreshments.

Friends of mine, married and living in Paris, have a regular arrangement with three other couples to meet every month and play a friendly session of duplicate bridge. Each couple receives in turn. With modest stakes, the losers pay into a kitty and the proceeds are used, for instance, to have an outing together to a top restaurant.

If you are not so fortunate to have a group of friends for bridge excursions abroad, there are also special bridge-at-sea luxury cruises which offer opportunities to play social and competitive bridge, with an on-board team of professionals to provide intermediate and advanced lessons to enthusiasts, with games every day. Generally, you can play as often, or as little, as you like. To select a bridge cruise, there are many websites, one of which is: www.betterbridge.com/cruises/index.html.

Now let's look at the main elements of the game.

SOME ESSENTIALS OF BRIDGE TERMINOLOGY

For readers who have no conception of how bridge is played, here are some of the main terms used in bridge.

Table

The game is played by a "table", made up of two teams, each with two partners who sit facing each other. Most bridge club sessions have multiple tables.

Players

The four players in any "deal" are named after the points of the compass. North sits facing their partner South and West faces their East partner, thus:

North

West   East

South

Deal

The word "deal" is used for two key elements of the game. As a verb, dealing the pack (or deck) of fifty-two cards to the four players, the thirteen cards to each player being called a "hand". And as a noun, for the entire process of play which ensues, bidding, playing out the cards, counting the tricks taken by each team and recording the score.

Tricks

Each trick consists of four cards. The highest value card, or if a player cannot follow suit, a "trump" card, wins the trick. Given that a pack has fifty-two cards, there are thirteen tricks per deal.

Trumps

Each deal has one suit denominated as "trumps", which outranks all other suits. This means that during any trick, if a player does not have any card of the suit of the opening card, that player can use any card from the trump suit and take the trick by "trumping".

No trumps

Depending on the successful bid, a deal can be designated as no trumps. That is exactly what it says, trumping is excluded from that particular deal.

Dummy

Once bidding (see below) is complete, the opening card of the deal is played, face up, by the person on the left of the "declarer", the player who initiated the successful bid. The declarer's partner becomes the "dummy" and places their cards face up on the table, arranged by suit. The declarer then proceeds to play both their hand and the dummy hand.

Ranking of suits

In bridge, the four suits of a card deck are given priority ranking for the purposes of the bidding process. Clubs are given the lowest ranking, followed by Diamonds, Hearts, and then Spades. A bid of no trumps is given the top rank.

Hand evaluation

For the purposes of bidding, each person evaluates their hand in accordance with a points system. An ace gets four points, a king three, a queen two and a jack one. Also the distribution of cards such as a void (no cards of a suit), a singleton (only one card of a suit), or a doubleton (only two cards of a suit) are taken into account for the points count evaluation.

This points count system for the bidding process originated in the 1960s, and was popularised by Charles Goren, the King of Aces.

Bidding and play

There are two distinct phases in each deal: bidding and playing out the cards with the "declarer" attempting to "make" his or her contract by winning at least the number of tricks bid and the opponents ("the defenders") striving to "defeat" the bid.

Bidding for contracts

In the first phase, the two opposing teams enter into an auction for the right to select the trump suit, with the winners making the highest bid for the number of tricks they can take if that suit is confirmed as trumps. Each bid is expressed as the number of tricks in excess of six out of the thirteen possible. Therefore, a bid of, say, one Club would require taking at least seven tricks with Clubs as trumps.

The end result of the bidding process for each deal is to award the contract to the team who has bid the highest number of tricks with a given suit as trumps or on a no trumps basis. When the deal is played out, points are awarded for success. If the contract fails, the opponents are awarded bonus points. Which is what bridge is all about. Successfully completing contracts or defeating them and accumulating sufficient points to win a complete session.

As each player announces a bid (or passes) during a given deal and players respond, an element of the content of the hands of each player is disclosed to all.

In effect, the bidding process of bridge involves subtle unspoken signals. For this reason, you and your partner have to agree on an understanding of the key elements of your mutual, unspoken communication for bidding, what are known as "conventions". The world of bridge has a number of established conventions which can be adopted by partners to send signals to each other during the bidding process.

A full understanding by you and your partner of the conventions that you will use is an essential part of the learning curve to establish an ongoing partnership between two players.

Play and how tricks are won

Let us assume that the North/South team has made a successful bid of, say, two Spades, that is, they have a contract to win at least eight tricks (6+2) with Spades as trumps.

The player to the left of South (the declarer), West plays an opening card, say, ace of Clubs, face up. North, the dummy, then places their hand face up on the table, arranged by suits. South will then play both their hand and the dummy hand.

The others follow, in clockwise order, South playing a card from the dummy hand of the same suit followed by East and then South. Let's say that South has no Clubs, and cannot "follow suit", then he/she is entitled to play a trump card, a Spade, and so wins the trick. South, as winner of the first trick will be in the lead for the second trick and so on until all thirteen cards of the deal are played out.

At this point, the scorer will tally the total tricks taken by each team and allocate points, either to the declarer if he has made his contract, or the opposing team if they were successful in defeating the contract.

RUBBER BRIDGE

Rubber bridge is generally a "social" gathering, with games being played amongst friends, either two couples or multiples of four people. With rubber bridge, hands dealt are played only once (unlike duplicate). Over a short period, therefore, the luck of the deal can influence the result. The first team to win two of three possible games is awarded a rubber. Players often change partners after each rubber, so that one gets to pair up with other members of the group.

DUPLICATE BRIDGE

Duplicate bridge, also called tournament bridge, involves multiple tables. The basics of duplicate bridge, that is, bidding for contracts and playing hands, are no different from rubber bridge, except that, with duplicate, the same hands dealt in the initial distribution of cards will be played by different players during the session. Thus, unlike rubber bridge, where being dealt good cards facilitates winning, one's final score at duplicate depends more on one's skill in bidding and playing of hands which are identical for all the competitors.

WHERE THE SATISFACTION OF BRIDGE LIES

Consistently playing well can be confirmation to many enthusiasts, especially those of a mature age bracket, that the mind is still alert and capable of analysing, deducing and executing and switching your game plan, as and when information arises.

To achieve this, you have to master the key elements of the game such as: applying correctly the applicable bidding convention to the hand you have been dealt (by no means an exact science); knowing when to stop or continue to bid, especially in competitive situations where both teams are vying for the contract; memorizing what cards have already been played, what winning cards remain and trying to guess who holds them.

GETTING STARTED

You can learn the basics of bridge by taking lessons from a competent player or, like many, by seeking guidance from playing with what an experienced bridge player friend of mine refers to as "a patient friend": perhaps that person who is trying to lure you into their bridge group or maybe your spouse. There are many books on learning bridge. Here are three:

Bridge for Beginners
    by Victor Mollo, Nico Gardener
Bridge for Dummies
    by Eddie Kantar
Bridge for Complete Beginners
    by Paul Mendelson

For those who are "into" computers, an excellent website for a clear insight into bridge is: www. retirementwithapurpose.com/bridge.html which leads you through the various elements of rubber bridge, the dealing, bidding and play, plus scoring. Then there is an introduction to duplicate bridge and the site finally provides links for playing bridge online if you feel up to it!

Irrespective of how you choose to learn, one necessity for all beginners is to become familiar with a few bidding conventions, but be careful, conventions change from country to country around the world. Top players have to learn lots of complex conventions, but, you'll be relieved to know, a moderate player can get by with a relatively few simple rules.

Once you have grasped the basics of bridge reasonably well, the next step is to find a partner, that is, in the absence of a playing spouse or that patient friend mentioned above. Even spouses are not always the ideal answer, since it is not unknown for a husband and wife to indulge in overt bickering over bidding and play, much to the embarrassment of others!

Finding a regular partner is probably the most difficult part for the lone beginner because tournament bridge clubs, by their very nature, are groupings of playing couples. Sometimes things do not work out with a beginner's first choice of playing partner, due to incompatible levels of competence, lack of coherence in bidding or whatever and perhaps you have try playing with someone else. A friendly bridge club president can help enormously by introducing you to someone who is either a beginner like yourself or another person who will lead you through the first few sessions until you find your feet. As with all human relations, time, patience and tolerance is the name of the game to find the ideal fit for a playing partner.

GOING FOR GOLD AT BRIDGE

A final word about what most players regard as the Holy Grail of bridge, a Grand Slam. This is where you and your partner both have dream hands and you have bid for seven of any suit or no trumps, and succeed.

That is, you take all thirteen tricks. Naturally, the points bonuses for such an achievement are maximum: kind of like scoring a hole in one at golf or kicking a winning goal in the last minute of extra time in a cup final.

But supposing you were only to take twelve tricks, in itself a remarkable feat, and fail to make your contract? Sorry, but the hammer falls and not only do you not gain any points but your opponents are awarded bonus points. As they say: that's life.

CHAPTER 3

Digging Up The Past

KNOWING MORE ABOUT PREHISTORIC MAN

Nowadays, more and more retired people are visiting famous archaeological sites at home and abroad to learn about ancient civilizations and compare their lives with our modern world. If you were to contemplate going on any trips to see for yourself the results gained from digging up the past, this chapter will set out some of the background knowledge of the science of archaeology which would give you a greater dimension of understanding what lies behind the sites. In this chapter you will find outlines of:

- how far back in the past man's origins have been traced
- some of our more evolved ancient civilizations
- techniques used by archaeologists and anthropologists in their research of man's evolution
- the various stepping stones in the evolution of homo sapiens since time began
- suggestions as to some interesting archaeological sites which might be worth visiting as an initiation to archaeology as an educational pastime.

PREHISTORIC ERA

The term prehistoric arose out of a system devised around the year 1800 by the curator of the National Museum of Denmark when he set about the task of classifying the museum's collection of artefacts by period of origin. He classified his prehistoric era as being time before history was extensively recorded in writing.

The Prehistoric era is divided into the following ages:

Stone age: 2.5 million to circa 4,000BC, split into three sub-periods:

Palaeolithic: 2.5 million BC to end of Ice Age 10,000BC

Mesolithic: transitional period between Ice Age and Neolithic

Neolithic: beginning of agriculture and domestication of animals, roughly 8,000 to 4,000BC.

Note: "-lithic" comes from the Greek word for "stone", "palaeo-" is derived also from Greek, meaning "ancient".

Bronze age: began in Greece and other Aegean countries in 4,000BC and ended around 1,200BC. In northern Europe it ended circa 800BC.

Iron age: ended around the fall of the Roman Empire c.475AD.

The most recent Ice Age is believed to have been started around 25,000 years ago and lasted a cool 15,000 years. The Ice Age prior to that was probably between 75,000 and 60,000 years ago. This data is derived from studies such as digs in the core of the Greenland ice cap but the accuracy of findings remain controversial. The origins of Ice Ages are complex but one factor is a periodic change in the Earth's tilt and annual orbiting pattern around the Sun – see chapter 9, Stargazing. During these Ice Ages, northern areas such as Britain and Scandinavia were covered in frozen snow to a depth of thousands of metres. When the last Ice Age terminated, the melting frozen crust flowed into the sea and sea levels surged upwards by some 120–130 metres (the height of a skyscraper) to what they are now. At present we are in an interglacial period.

Why not read more about the Stone and Ice Age with:

Dark Caves, Bright Visions: Life in Ice Age Europe
  by Randall White
The Lost Civilizations of the Stone Age
  by Richard Rudgley

SOME OF THE GREAT PREHISTORIC CIVILIZATIONS

The earliest civilizations, which have yielded considerable archaeological treasures, all surrounded the Mediterranean during the prehistoric era at a time when northern Europeans were primitive people living in caves and mud-huts. These civilizations were Egypt, Greece and the Roman Empire. You may rightly say: but everybody knows that! Well, if you are going to take a deeper interest in archaeology, it might be best to jog your memory of what you learned in your Miss McKinnon's history class in your halcyon teenage days.

Egypt

Egypt's era of glory in early times dates back to roughly 3,000BC when nomadic tribes gathered in the fertile Nile valley and set up their village communities. Historians split ancient Egypt, ruled by the pharaohs, into three Kingdoms.

The first period, the Old Kingdom, spanned 2,600 to 2,100BC, with Memphis, just south of Cairo, as its main city and religious centre.

This was what historians term the Pyramid Age. Two types of pyramid were built during this period. The first, a "step" pyramid, which has several platform levels rising to a flat top, was built in Saqqara near Memphis, a construction made entirely of stone.

The other more classic-shaped pyramids were first built around 2,575BC, the most famous being the Great Pyramid of Khufu, also called Cheops, at Giza, near Cairo. Until the age of the skyscrapers in New York in the 1920s, the Khufu pyramid, with its height of over 230 metres, was amongst the tallest structures in the world and one of the seven wonders of the world. It was a gigantic project, even more so in those early days of architecture and building construction. Around 100,000 men are said to have been employed, assembling limestone and granite rocks weighing two to three tons each, some of up to nine tons. It is reckoned that, in all, around 2.3 million blocks of stone went into putting up the Great Pyramid of Khufu.

Can you imagine moving these hunks of rock without the aid of a crane?

The methods used are still a subject of much speculation but most researchers now agree that probably ramps, running diagonally from the ground to the each top level, were built and the boulders manhandled up the ramps on sledges, with the ramps later dismantled, like scaffolding is today, when each stage was complete. The human casualty rate through accident and muscular stress must have been horrendous.

In these early days of collective labour, the workers had no choice but to accept to be treated as mules. But the

Egyptians, give them their due, are on record as being the first ever to declare a strike. The strike took place in the 12th century BC during the construction of Rameses III's tomb in Thebes (see below) when the workers walked off site; not it seems as a protest against working conditions but simply because they had not been fed. One has to assume that being fed was their sole motivation to work quite apart from fear of flogging.

The pharaohs were not unique in exploiting fellow human beings for organized labour. It took another 4,000 years, to be more precise, not until the 19th century during the Industrial Revolution in Europe, before trade unions were legally recognized by governments.

Standing beside the Great Pyramid of Khufu, (or Cheops) are the pyramids of Khafre (or Chepren), Khufu's son, and of Menkaure, believed to be Khufu's grandson. They seem to have been a family with a bent for self-indulgence, especially if you add the Sphinx, at Giza alongside the pyramid of Khafre, built by Khafre as a second monument to his father, Khufu.

The Middle Kingdom, 2,040 to 1,640BC is now seen as the height of ancient Egyptian intellectual development and culture.

The New Kingdom, 1,550 to 1,070BC, had its capital in Thebes about 700 kilometres south of Cairo, on the Nile, and boasted the richest monuments of all, with temples at Karnak and Luxor and the luxurious tombs of royalty in the Valley of the Kings, a veritable mine for discoveries by latter day archaeologists.

It is interesting to note that the obelisk, which stands in the centre of the Place de la Concorde in Paris, was transported from Luxor as part of the spoils of Napoleon's military campaign in Egypt during 1798–99.

One of the best known faces of Egyptology is that of

the beautiful queen pharaoh, Nerfeti, who ruled during the New Kingdom. A limestone bust of Nerfeti, known as Egypt's Sun Queen, was first exhibited in Berlin in 1924, launching the fame of her beauty. Nerfeti's sarcophagus (stone coffin) is one of the few burial remains of Pharaohs never to have been found and thus is high on the list of prime targets for new digs.

To read more about Nerfeti and her times:

Nerfeti Lived Here
by Mary Chubb, a British archaeologist who spent most of her life digging up the past in the Middle East and who was a regular broadcaster for the BBC, before her death, at 99, in 2003.

Another interesting read about the female face of ancient Egypt is:

Hatchepsut: The Female Pharaoh
by Joyce Tyldesley, also a well known British archaeologist. Queen Hatchepsut's famous temple is situated at Luxor.

Greece and the Aegean

The earliest Greek civilization was that of the Minoans who lived mainly in Crete, that gorgeous Mediterranean island in the sun. Earliest records indicate that the Minoans, like the Egyptians, also date back to c.3,000BC. Their refined living was first revealed by the excavations by teams led by Sir Arthur Evans at Knossos, between 1900 and 1935. The Minoans reached their peak during the late Bronze Age with palaces in Knossos, Phaistos, Zakro and Mallia, all notable for their sumptuous art and architecture.

Around 1,600BC, the Minoan civilization dispersed in the aftermath of earthquakes, followed by volcanic eruptions, possibly on the island of Thera (also called Santorini), creating huge tidal waves and hot ash falling over a wide area, devastating Crete.

Excavations at Akrotiri in Thera/Santorini have now been underway since 1967 by teams from the Archaeological Society of Athens to probe into the theory that the volcanic eruption was in fact responsible for the collapse of the Minoan civilization. The isle of Thera, due north of Crete is a wonderful place to visit to learn more about the Bronze Age Minoans and the science of digging up the past.

More recently, interest in Akrotiri has been heightened by suggestions that the site might have had some connection with the mythical sub-continent of Atlantis, described in the writings of the scholar Plato (427–347BC).

Atlantis, generally thought to have lain west of what the ancient Greeks called the Pillars of Hercules (straits of Gibraltar) in the Atlantic Ocean, was said to have been a beautiful and prosperous island state, which once ruled parts of Europe and Africa and, according to legend, later sunk below the ocean.

Profiting from the widespread chaos of the Minoan misfortunes, the Mycenaens took over power in Greece and established over the next two centuries prosperous cities in Mycenae, with an ancient fortress, in the Peleponnese, Tiryns and Pylos, with beautiful palaces. Artefacts – man-made objects such as tools, weapons, cups and bowls – of gold, ivory and inlaid bronze of exquisite design were, during the 18th and 19th centuries, excavated from tombs of Mycenaen royalty and are now on show to the public in the Athens archaeological museum. The end of the Mycenaen supremacy took place with the general dispersion of its people during the end of the Bronze Age, c.1,200BC after an invasion by the Dorians from the north, armed with weapons made of iron in contrast to the softer bronze used by the Mycenaens.

From that date onward, Greece continued to develop a unique civilization with the coming to power of the Dorians, who spoke Doric (a word used nowadays by the Scots to mean dialect!) which was akin to Greek. It was during this period in Greek history that, in 776BC, the first Olympic games were held with contestants coming from great city-states such as Athens and Sparta.

Greek history: real life or poetry?

The most fascinating aspect of prehistoric Greek history is that of myths intermixed with real life events. Most of the Greek myths are recorded by poets such as Homer and Hesiod, dating back to circa 700BC and later, by the Roman poet, Virgil (70–19BC).

The many myths or legends include deity like the all-powerful Zeus, god of the sky; Aphrodite, goddess of love; Dionysus, god of wine; Poseidon, of earthquakes and the sea; and Apollo, son of Zeus and god of the arts and medicine. In the Greek world, the gods did not create man, man created the gods. All their gods looked like humans, but, naturally, were more beautiful and gifted, and the most powerful lived at the court of Zeus on the mythical Mount Olympus. Temples were built for the best known, notably Athena, the patron goddess of Athens, in whose honour the Parthenon, with its 46 Doric columns, was constructed in the 5th century BC and built on the Acropolis, the upper, fortified part of Athens.

Amongst the many enigmas facing historians and

archaeologists, the most intriguing and romantic is whether the Trojan War was fact or fiction.

Legend has it that the ten-year Trojan War was a combat between the Greeks of Sparta, in Mycenae, and the citizens of Troy, thought to be in what is now Turkey and situated on the northeast coast of the Aegean Sea. The tale of the Trojan War is from Homer's poetry, The Iliad, with a follow-on in his 24-book epic poem, Odyssey.

Here is a synopsis of the war. In an arrangement brokered by Aphrodite, Paris, younger son of King Priam of Troy, on a visit to Sparta, fell in love with the wife of Menelaus, King of Sparta, the beautiful Helen, she who had "the face that launched a thousand ships". And the young lovers fled to Troy, taking with them much treasure.

An angered King Menelaus promptly arranged a fleet of the thousand ships and a vast army of warriors, led by his brother, Agamemnon and including many famous Greek heros, notably Achilles, of "Achilles heel" fame, and Odysseus, who came alive in Homer's Odyssey, when, at the end of the Trojan war, he had an amorous affair with one Calypso, a nymph who kept him on her island for seven years, and had many other adventures of poetic fantasy.

The citadel of Troy proved to be impenetrable to the fierce onslaught of the Spartans until Agamemnon hit on the brilliant ploy of the now legendary Trojan Horse, allowing his warriors to enter the city. Achilles slew Hector, the top Trojan warrior, elder son of King Priam but died later from an arrow wound, of course, in his heel, from the bow of Paris. The Greeks finally sacked and destroyed the city by fire.

To read more about Troy, here are a couple of suggestions:

The Iliad (Wordsworth Classics)
  by Homer
In Search of the Trojan War
  by Michael Wood

For the last sixteen years, a team of three-hundred and fifty scholars, scientists and technicians from twenty countries and led by a German archaeologist, has been working on excavations at a site in Hisarlik in northwestern Turkey, believed to be the remains of Troy.

This site was first discovered by Heinrich Schliemann, another German archaeologist, who began excavations as far back as 1871. Schliemann, a successful businessman, only took up archaeology at the age of 50, after studying the science in Paris. From Hisarlik, Schliemann moved on to Mycenae in 1876 where his team uncovered many fabulous artefacts, including two gold death-masks which he claimed, probably out of self-aggrandizement, were those from the tomb of King Agamemnon of Troy fame. More prudently, these are now labelled as 'known as the mask of Agamemnon' at the Athens archaeological museum. Yet another illustration of the intrigues of archaeology: the finder's conclusions as to the origins of relics dating back to prehistoric times often being subject to controversy and counter claims.

To learn more about Agamemnon and Mycenae, read The Tomb of Agamemnon by Cathy Gere, an academic specializing in ancient history, a work which also provides a detailed explanation of the site at Mycenae for those intending to pay a visit.

Ancient Greece came to an end in a blaze of glory under Alexander the Great (356–323BC) of Macedonia, who was a pupil of the great philosopher, Aristotle. One of the greatest military leaders of all time, he led his armies to conquer present-day Afghanistan and Pakistan, Egypt, other parts of northern Africa and southern Europe before dying of malaria at Babylon at the early age of 33. He was buried in a beautiful tomb in Alexandria, Egypt. Three centuries later Greece became part of the Roman Empire.

Suggested viewing: Oliver Stone's 2005 film, Alexander, with Colin Farrel in the star role and Sir Anthony Hopkins as Ptolemy, astronomer and one of the greatest of Greek philosophers, and who is mentioned in chapter 9, Stargazing.

The Roman Empire

The period shortly before the transition from BC to AD saw the rise and dominance of the Roman Empire over a vast area of the Old World stretching from Armenia and Mesopotamia (now Iraq) in the east, to the Iberian peninsula in the west, including Greece; the entire north Africa from Egypt to what is now Morocco; from central Europe which was at that time Gaul (basically France and Belgium) to the Rhine valley and the Danube in the east; and a part of Britain from its southern coastline up to what is today the lowlands of Scotland.

Thus you have a pan-European empire built by Rome, not so much by scholars, architects and philosophers but by the sword and which endured almost constant wars against insurgent tribes over the entire empire, and political in-fighting for power in Rome where few emperors ever died a peaceful death.

The Roman Empire lasted for roughly 500 years with its demise in 476AD when the last emperor Romulus Augustulus stepped down in the wake of massive attacks by the Visigoths and the Vandals, both formidable

Germanic tribes, on major parts of the Empire including North Africa, Spain and Gaul. The Visigoths settled in Aquitaine in SW France. This insurgency resulted in the withdrawal of the Roman power from these countries and culminated in the sacking of Rome by the Vandals in 455AD.

To add to the scenario of constant insurgency across Europe during the Roman Empire, concurrent with their offensive against the Romans, the Visigoths themselves were on the run towards the west from the invading Huns, not German as used in today's derogatory language, but fierce tribesmen from Asia, led by the renowned Attila.

The Romans occupied most of Britain, except the far north, from 67AD onwards. This was after the defeat of the resistance led by the gallant Queen Boadicea who led her insurgent army against the invaders and sacked Colchester, St Albans and London before being routed by superior forces led by the governor Paulinus.

During their occupation of Britain, the Romans built the Antonine Wall between the Firth of Forth and the Firth of Clyde to try to contain the continual attacks from the fierce tribal Picts who inhabited the unconquered northern Scotland. By 181AD, the Picts had forced the Romans to build, and retreat to behind Hadrian's Wall which stretched between the Solway Firth in the west and the mouth of the river Tyne in the east. In 407AD, in tandem with their retreat throughout rest of Europe, the Romans withdrew their forces from Britain, after occupying a large part of the country for almost 400 years.

All in all, the Roman Empire was a turbulent and war torn era but which left in its wake a splendid pan-European infrastructure of roads and towns.

Some suggested reading:

Britain and the End of the Roman Empire
  by Ken Dark
The Roman Empire, 27BC to AD476: A Study in Survival
  by Chester G. Starr
The End of the Western Roman Empire: An Archaeological Investigation
  by Ellen Swift

MEGALITHIC SITES

For the most part of the prehistoric era, civilizations around the globe erected megalithic sites – from the Greek "megas"-great, "lithos"-stone – places having large stones, some weighing several tons and arranged in mysterious ways. Little is known of the *raison d'être* of such sites and the logic of positioning of the stones. Historians and archaeologists advance theories on a site-by-site basis of the worship of ancient gods, honouring burial grounds and what some term "archaeoastronomy", aligning stones according to positions of the sun and moon at certain times of the year such as summer and winter solstices.

Notable examples of megalithic sites in Europe are Stonehenge on the Salisbury Plains in England, discussed later, and Carnac, in northwest France, where there are over 3,000 stones arranged in avenues, the largest megalithic site in the world. Nearby, at Locmariaquer lies the Tumulus d'Er-Grah, a megalith, now lying horizontal in four pieces, perhaps the world's tallest. When standing, it was twenty metres high and adjoins a Neolithic tumulus ("tumulus" means ancient burial mound).

THE HISTORY OF ARCHAEOLOGY

Archaeology is a fairly recent pursuit, if one considers that learning in the western world began in earnest during the 14th century, the dawn of the Renaissance in Europe.

The probing of knowing more about how man lived in the past, by studying megalithic sites and excavations, began in Europe only around the early 1800s. Prior to then, there had been much romantic speculation by historians as to ancient civilizations but no systematic delving into the past, as archaeologists now practice the science, with pick and shovel, albeit delicately applied, or by studying the form of pottery, tools, weapons and other artefacts.

During the 20th century, compensating for its slow coming of age, archaeology advanced rapidly in several directions:

- development of methodology, including teaming of experts such as palaeontologists, botanists and geologists, to seek meaning out of archaeological remains
- formation of special branches of the art, such as marine and industrial
- use of scientific aids, like aerial photography or radio-carbon dating, to assist investigations.

Excavation analysis

Early in the history of archaeology, there was the emergence of what is now technically called stratigraphy which is the term given to the skilled interpretation of the sequence of each of a series of layers or strata of rocks or clay revealed by excavation. Layers can indicate phases of reconstruction, periods of abandonment and so on.

That is precisely where the interest in archaeology lies. Like journalism, the challenge is to find out the story behind a bland picture, in archaeology's case, a picture given by artefacts, fossils, ruins, and excavated strata of rock and earth.

For instance, at the site mentioned earlier, the one in Hisarlik in Turkey, suspected as being ancient Troy, analysis of excavation findings has concluded that it started its existence as an early Bronze Age citadel around 3,000BC and ended up as a Byzantine (eastern Roman Empire, known for its complicated and devious ways of governing) settlement prior to abandonment. Evidence of a massive and destructive fire, a few skeletons and primitive weapons point to a battle, if not the war, which is what the archaeological exercise is mainly about.

Excavations also indicate that the site at Hisarlik had been a city of importance, a citadel unmatched anywhere in the eastern Mediterranean as guardian of the route between the Aegean and the Black Sea and therefore worthy of a large-scale war; which concurs with the story as unfolded by Homer's The Iliad.

A possibility to join in excavation sites

The international scientific research organization and charity, Earthwatch Institute, has research teams working on many archaeological sites around the world and welcomes small numbers of members of the public as visiting students.

You could visit, on a paid basis, one of Earthwatch's sites for ten days to two weeks, to be actively involved with field researchers in the excavations, and attend evening talks about geology, palaeontology and the archaeology of the area. Note that these visits are not entirely holidays but a hands-on introduction to archaeology.

An example of the kind of site open to visits.

Earthwatch has had a team working on a site in Orce, in the province of Granada in Andalucia since 1976, studying the last four million years of geological history in the area and the presence of some species of man, possibly homo erectus, dating back to perhaps 1.5 million years. Members of the public are welcome to join the team, no previous experience required, only a keen interest in learning more about the past.

Another intriguing site that I noted when surfing the Earthwatch website is in Romania, in a spot called Halmyris, close to the delta of the Danube. There, the Earthwatch team is uncovering the remains of ancient Greek and Roman civilizations.

More information on Earthwatch is available in chapter 6, Protecting the Planet. To learn about available paid stays at their many archaeological sites worldwide, either contact Earthwatch Institute (Europe) in Oxford or, if you can, log on to their website www.earthwatch.org where you will find lots of intelligence on this splendid global environmental organization.

Studying changes in form of objects

Another interesting term used in archaeology is typology. This describes the art of expert evaluation of changes in the form and design of ancient objects such as artifacts, weapons, pottery and tools, which can link discoveries at one archaeological site to another.

EXPERTS IN ARCHAEOLOGY

Now let's have a look at the various skills of the specialists in digging up the past.

First, there are the anthropologists who study man's social organization and cultures. Then there are the palaeontologists who study life during the Stone Age. Anatomists examine human and animal fossils, extrapolate on who they were, try to reconstruct what they looked like way back when they were alive and what they were up to during their lifetimes. The botanists, whose science dates back to the Greek scholars around 300BC, give expert advice on plant remains on sites. And, of course, geologists are brought in to give opinions on the possible history of rocks and other earth substances found by excavation.

Special divisions of archaeology

Modern archaeology puts marine activities, exploration and discovery of ancient shipwrecks and studies of sites at the bottom of the ocean littered with sunken vessels, in a category of their own, since the geographical know-how, techniques and equipment required are so specialized.

There is also industrial archaeology, which deals with the study of early buildings, machines and methods of communication of, for example, the Industrial Revolution in Europe which commenced in the second half of the 18th century.

Dating fossils

Whilst fossils for animals and plants are being dug up all the time, human fossils are extremely rare. This is explained by the extraordinary conditions required if a corpse buried centuries ago is to turn up on an excavation site as a fossil. The cadaver has to have been buried in a sediment such as sand or earth and seeped in water which later solidified it over a period of time into a rock-like substance before decomposition of the bones. When, however, the excavation unearths the remains, perhaps fossilized, of what was obviously a human, the key question arises as to how long this particular corpse has been dead. This is where carbon 14 detection, or to give it its formal name radio-carbon dating, comes in.

In the 1940s, researchers discovered the existence of what is known as carbon 14. All living things absorb carbon, either from breathing in the carbon dioxide in the air or by eating plants that contain it. Once an animal or human being dies, the proportion of carbon 14 in the remains drops steadily and, by measuring the concentration of this vital substance in the corpse, experts can put a fairly approximate finger on the date of decease, because it is reckoned that, after 5,500 years, one half of the carbon 14 has dissipated. And after a further 5,500 years all traces of carbon are exhausted.

THE ORIGINS AND EVOLUTION OF MAN

So, what are some of the more important findings about man's origins and evolution since time began? Although our religious teachings indicate the contrary, scientific research dates man's origins to apes in Africa some 4.5 million years ago. Some 300,000 years later, these future humans adopted a semi-upright stance. From then on a steady evolutionary process took the apes to what is called homo habilus, followed perhaps some 1.5 million years ago by homo erectus, man standing upright on two feet. Homo erectus was also living outside of Africa since the oldest human fossils ever to be found, perhaps as old as 800,000 years, a homo erectus, were dug up near Trinil in Java in 1891 and called the Java man.

Prehistoric homo sapiens

The species of man beginning to resemble the most today's human beings goes back some 80,000 years and, as we all know, is called homo sapiens. It appears that the existence of homo sapiens was limited to Africa up until about 75,000 years ago. So how did homo sapiens come to burgeon around the globe? The answer seems to be that about 60,000 years ago homo sapiens migrated from Africa by crossing the straits at the southern end of the Red Sea to the Middle East and from there dispersed eastwards into Asia and on through SE Asia to Australia. One major setback in South East Asia to any specimens of humanity could have been the greatest ever volcanic eruption, at Toba in Sumatra, which devastated a vast area of the Far East with thick layers of ash as far as northern Pakistan. The eruption caused a large area to subside forming a caldera one hundred kilometres long and thirty kilometres wide creating Lake Toba with its island Samosir. Looking to the western hemisphere, the first homo sapiens to settle in Europe probably came via central Asia and the Middle East some 35,000 years ago.

The Neanderthals

The first fossils of prehistoric man to be discovered in Europe belonged to the Neanderthal man, so-called because he was found, in 1856, in a valley of that name, located in Germany, near Dusseldorf. Another Neanderthal skeleton was unearthed in the early 1900s in France, at La Chatelle-aux-Saints in the Dordogne. (For unknown reasons, the Dordogne in southwest France is the "in" place for archaeological discoveries of prehistoric man's fossils).

These early specimens of homo sapiens lived between 300,000 and 30,000 years ago, mainly in Europe and Asia.

The Neanderthals had, according to the anatomists who have "reconstructed" the body, prominent eyebrow ridges, a narrow skull, and a protruding upper jaw with a short chin, and were deep-chested.

The Cro-Magnons

The real beginnings of modern homo sapiens who followed in the footsteps of the Neanderthals, is called the Cro-Magnon man who lived between 35,000 and 10,000 years ago and was named after the location where first found, in France, yet again in the Dordogne.

The Cro-Magnons lived throughout Europe during the Ice Age. They were virtually identical to what we are today, being tall and strong to survive the rigorous conditions of freezing temperatures and nomadic hunting to survive, with similar levels of intelligence.

Indeed it is said that, were you to give a Cro-Magnon man a wash and shave, put him in a suit and stick him on the London Underground, you would not be able to identify him from the rest of the crushed, married and mortgaged urban commuters, except that, sad to say, the wash, shave and decent suit would probably make him stand out in the crowd.

The Cro-Magnons are famous for their fine artwork such as ivory carvings, mostly of humans and animals, musical instruments and above all, their wonderful cave paintings.

The paintings on the walls and ceilings of their caves were done with manganese and iron oxide, dissolved in, interestingly, saliva. This discovery was made by France's National Centre for Scientific Research who surmise rather poetically that the Cro-Magnons were convinced that spitting was a way of projecting themselves into the work of art and becoming personified with the animal or hunter they were painting!

GO AND SEE FOR YOURSELF

With that brief outline of archaeology, here are some suggestions of options for on-site visits as pleasant holidays. There are also ideas for reading in advance to gather more detail of what you should be looking for when you get there.

So, first let's take Egypt and Thebes whose principal town, Luxor, is located on the banks of the Nile, about 700 kilometres south of Cairo. This is a huge complex with Karnak and its temple of Amun and the Valley of the Kings with the remains of the temple of Hatshepsut in Luxor, alongside the tombs of the ancient pharaohs. For those burials, the ancient Egyptians practiced their renowned skills of mummifying the bodies of their rulers by a dehydration process using resins, bandages and decoration.

It is in the Valley of the Kings where you find the tomb of Tutankhamun, popularly known as King Tut, world famous for the dazzling treasures, including the gold funeral mask, found when the site, untouched by man since 1,325BC, was unearthed by a team led by the British archaeologist Howard Carter in 1922. King Tut had no fame as a pharaoh, since he died at the early age of seventeen, but the impeccable state of the tomb and its exquisite treasures make the find probably the greatest archaeological discovery of Egyptology. There has been much speculation as to how he died. Was it murder or death by natural causes? The fabulous King

Tut jewellery, statues and sculptures are on view at the Egyptian Museum in Cairo.

Egypt is an ideal place for an introduction to archaeology and provides an opportunity to profit from a holiday cruise on the Nile.

Suggested reading:

Luxor: Guide to Ancient Thebes by Jill Kamil
Tutankhamun by Aude Gros de Beler

Or, why not visit Greece and the site of Mycenae, situated on a small hilltop on the road from the Argolic Gulf to Corinth, with Athens further north, and which contains relics of the civilization who ruled mainland Greece in the late Bronze Age, 1,400 to 1,200BC. Tiryns, another main settlement of the Mycenaens, is nearby, slightly further south. The acropolis (the fortified walls of ancient Greek cities) of Mycenae overlooks a ravine as a defence against attackers.

Mycenae is a great place to visit, especially since it is in a beautiful part of the Greek coastline and not too far from Athens with its Parthenon and other marvelous treasures including the National Archaeological Museum.

Suggested reading:

Greece: From Mycenae to the Parthenon
  by Henri Stierlin

Another choice for a visit to ancient Greece is Delphi, situated about 100 kilometres from Athens, overlooking the sea of the Gulf of Corinth, on the forested slopes of Mount Parnassus. One of the most important religious sanctuaries of ancient Greece, the spot was dedicated to Apollo, son of Zeus. It was the seat of the Delphic Oracle where Pythia, the priestess of Apollo, in a state of ecstasy induced by fragrant smoke, replied to questions regarding the future. Excavations have revealed that the site was a Mycenaen village during 1,500–1,100BC. Many ruins include the temple of Apollo dating back to the 4th century BC.

Suggested reading:

The Oracle of Delphi
   by Elizabeth Rose

Nothing quite symbolizes the power and cruelty of the Roman Empire as much as the ruins of the Colosseum in the romantic city of Rome, with its beautiful piazzas and lovely people sitting eating delicious pasta and sipping chianti wine in pavement cafés, all talking volubly at the same time. What a splendid city to visit.

In 1829, the French novelist, Henri Stendahl, in his *Promenades dans Rome*, wrote "What wonderful mornings I have spent in the Colosseum, lost in some corner of these vast ruins" and suggested that the Colosseum was more attractive in ruins than it may have been when active.

The Colosseum was opened by the Emperor Titus in 79AD during a period when the empire was in a state of chaos caused by war on all sides. The Romans built some 250 amphitheatres all over their empire but the Colosseum was the largest of all with space for 50,000 spectators, to watch gladiators (who were mostly slaves) indulge in combat to the death with lions and leopards.

Suggested reading:

The Age of the Gladiators
   by Rupert Matthews

Or, why not study up on the history of Hadrian's Wall,

started in 122AD to keep the barbarian Scots out of England during the Roman occupation, and visit some of the more significant sections between the Solway Firth in the west and the mouth of the river Tyne in the east?

Suggested reading:

Hadrian's Wall
  by D J Breeze

For those readers with an interest in paintings and drawings, a visit to the cave site at Altamira in Santillana del Mar (Cantabria), Spain, just south of Santander on the northwest coastline facing the Atlantic, would be well worthwhile.

The cueva de Altimira, as it is called in Spanish, is the remnants of the Magdalenian people, now famous for their roof and wall paintings of hunting scenes of bison, wild boars, horses and deer. The Magdalenians lived during c.15,000 to 11,000BC, around the same time as the Cro-Magnons and are so-called because they were first discovered at a site at La Madelaine, also in the Dordogne, ever the hub for palaeolithic cave paintings.

The Magdalenian paintings are in natural earth pigments such as ochre and zinc oxides producing as many as three colours of the body of each animal, and are reckoned by the experts to have been done by early homo sapiens 14,000 years ago at the zenith of cave art.

Access to the cave itself is restricted in order to conserve the paintings with state-of-the-art climatic conditions, but what is referred to as a "neo-cave" has been meticulously reproduced on site, using the same painting techniques to provide a realistic impression of the originals for public appreciation.

Suggested reading:

The Cave of Altamira
  by Antonio Beltran

You could also visit a couple of the Cro-Magnon sites in France. One famous site, the caves at Lascaux, near Sarlat in the Dordogne, contains spectacular drawings of antelope, bulls and horses painted some 16,000 years ago during the Ice Age. The caves also are testimony of prehistoric man's interest in the cosmos, since they contain an etching of a map of the Pleiades star cluster, called the Seven Sisters, in the Taurus constellation, stars which could then, and today can be viewed with the naked eye.

The other site worth a visit is the prehistoric cave at La Marche located in Lussac-les-Chateaux, near Montmorillon which is in the region of Poitiers. La Marche was in the news a few years ago because of the hundreds of drawings of human faces discovered carved on limestone slabs covering the floor of the cave. If these etchings are genuinely prehistoric, done around 15,000 years ago, then they could well rate as the earliest portraits of human faces ever found, dating back to long before, for example, the symbolic face carved into a boulder at Stonehenge.

And finally, why not visit Stonehenge, much nearer home for British readers and the "Big Daddy" of all unsolved mysteries of megaliths, set on the Salisbury Plains in Southern England.

Stonehenge was built in three stages over a period between 3,100 and 1,500BC, that is, during the Bronze Age, over 2,000 years before the Romans arrived in Britain. No one seems to know how and why this monument of boulders was put in place. Some theory leans towards the view that it was a place of worship, which makes sense. Only deity could incite an undertaking of such mammoth proportions. What is known is that some of the huge stones, weighing around four tons and more, required a lot of muscle power in those days, thousands of years before fork-lift trucks and cranes.

It is believed that the massive boulders were hauled on sledges with wooden runners by armies of men over ground and by raft on river, some all the way from a quarry at Mount Prescelly in Wales, a distance of 300 miles to the site at Stonehenge. Stonehenge is indeed eloquent testimony to the ingenuity of prehistoric man.

Suggested reading:

Stonehenge Complete
  by Christopher Chippindale

And to learn about some of the megalithic sites and other remains of ancient civilizations around the world not mentioned in this chapter, a superb read is:

The Atlas of Mysterious Places
  edited by Jennifer Westwood

Another entertaining way to cultivate your appetite to know more about man's life since prehistoric times is to tune into the BBC programmes on archaeological mysteries from around the world, presented by Aubrey Manning, retired Professor of Natural History, University of Edinburgh, in his series Unearthing Mysteries on Radio 4. Here are but a few examples of the diversity and geography of subjects covered. Professor Manning has travelled to Egypt to tour the legendary Land of Punt, a vast expanse around the Red Sea where trade by ancient Egyptians took place, and visit the temple of the female pharaoh Hatsepsut dating back to around 1,470BC. He has entertained listeners to an account of recently found cave art, ultra rare for Britain, with engravings of a deer stag, birds and bisons, at Cresswell Crags in Nottinghamshire. And he took his listeners to an abandoned quarry in Mexico where suspected human footprints, possibly 40,000 years old and preserved in hardened volcanic ash, were found by a team from Liverpool John Moores University, giving rise to speculation that homo sapiens may have crossed from Siberia to the Americas 40,000 years ago, in the global migration from Africa; much earlier than ever thought possible.

If you have access to the internet, you can review written accounts of past presentations of Unearthing Mysteries on the BBC website by keying in "Aubrey Manning" at Explore and clicking on Search.

What is offered in this chapter is only a glimpse of archaeology and the history of ancient civilizations. This could be the start of a long period of enjoyment and occupation for you, the reader, to learn more through reading, listening to experts and on-site visits to see for yourself the forms of society, ways of life and the skills in art, architecture and the making of tools and weapons for hunting of our very early ancestors.

As you study in more depth ancient civilizations, you might reflect on how our ancestral fellow human beings carved out their happiness in day-to-day life, developed means to improve living conditions and coped with hardships such as primitive health care in often extreme climates such as ice ages, wars and famine. By contrast, who knows, it might also just make you feel a shade happier with life in the 21st century, or wryly surmise that we should learn from history, change our ways and go back to our roots.

CHAPTER 4

Bobby Fischer, Move Over

ENTERING THE WONDERFUL WORLD OF CHESS

Chess is a truly universal game. Anywhere in the world you may find enthusiasts who will accept with pleasure a chance to pit their skills against your own, over a chessboard which knows neither cultural nor language frontiers.

Age is not an obstacle to taking up chess. Indeed, it is quite common for those who gave up the game early in life to take it up again when they retire and be pleasantly surprised to find that they actually become more skilful than in their youth. Chess is an excellent exercise for the ageing brain.

Chess is also a great family pastime. Fathers enjoy taking on their sons or daughters in a game of chess or, even better, grandfathers playing against their grandchildren. Imagine the pleasure of playing against a grandchild just starting to learn – and the mutual delight when he or she latches on to the game and starts to beat grandad! I would add that, for some odd reason, chess has traditionally been a male prerogative but, in today's world, more and more women are to be found playing the game.

CHESS THROUGH THE AGES

The roots of chess go back to around fifteen hundred

years ago to India, where it was a board game depicting two opposing armies, from whence it moved to Persia.

During the 8th century, the Moors invaded and conquered southern Spain, bringing with them chess from Persia. Cordoba, under Moorish rule, over the next seven centuries grew to become a great city. Over that period, scholars from northern countries visited Cordoba to learn medicine, science, philosophy and the arts and, through these seekers of knowledge, chess spread northwards across Europe.

Over the ensuing centuries, chess gained popularity worldwide. Italy led the rest of Europe in playing skills during the 17th century. In the 18th century it was France's turn to produce chess masters, with the Café de la Régence in Paris, situated near the Louvre, as the world's chess centre, where eminences such as Benjamin Franklin, Voltaire, Robespierre and Napoleon, in his younger days, played.

During the mid-Victorian era, London was a centre of excellence with chess masters like Staunton, Burn, and Blackburne. In 1834, a series of matches were held in London between England's best player, McDonnell and de la Bourdonnais, the French national champion, who won the series. The matches are considered a milestone in the history of the game and were recorded and made available to a wide public in book form and analysed by leading masters. The first international tournament was also held in London, in 1851, and was won by Anderssen, a German national champion.

A MOMENT TO LEARN

There is an oft quoted saying about chess, "a moment to learn; a lifetime to master". Let's therefore take a moment to look at the basics of the game as played the world over.

Setting up the board

A chessboard has 64 individual squares, 32 dark and 32 light. The two opposing chess players each have sixteen pieces, one player the white pieces, the other the black. These sixteen pieces are composed of, in ranking order: one king; one queen; two bishops; two knights; two rooks (or castles); and eight pawns. They are arranged on opposing sides of the board as follows:

The queen (with the five ° above crown) stands on a square of her own colour and the king (with the + above crown) on a square of his opposite colour. The above line-up leaves 32 vacant squares between the two opposing armies before the initial advances. Once the game is started, play takes place on all 64 squares.

HOW THE PIECES MOVE

The movement of pawns can be likened to that of foot soldiers. For the most part, the pawns can only advance one square at a time in a straight line, never to retreat, with the role of sacrificing their lives to weaken the adversary. There are two exceptions to this one square/ straight line rule. Each pawn can advance two squares for its first move. And they move diagonally one square to capture an opposing piece if that piece is in a square diagonally adjacent. Note that capture is not permitted if the opposing piece is in a vertical or horizontal square adjacent to the pawn.

If ever a pawn reaches the opponent's base line intact, the reward is high. The plucky pawn can be exchanged (or "promoted") for a more premium piece, generally a queen, the most valuable of all. Such a promotion is generally enough to win the game outright, unless, of course, the opponent manages to promote one of their own pawns.

The rooks, or castles which they resemble, can move any number of squares, either vertically or horizontally but cannot jump over another piece or move diagonally. Rooks can capture any opposing piece facing it directly in any vertical or horizontal square.

Knights, which resemble a horse's head, are the only pieces which are allowed to hop over other pieces, moving two squares in a straight line in any direction and then one square to the side, in an "L" movement. If the knight lands on a square containing an opponent's piece, the piece is captured. Note that the knight changes the colour of its square each time it moves.

The knights have an advantage over all other pieces in that their hopping ability allows them to make opening moves right at the start of the game whereas the rooks, bishops, queen and king all have to wait until a pawn moves to clear a passage to advance. On the other hand, they can only move short distances and thus take longer to cross the board. This is why knights generally move early in the game towards the centre of the board where the action tends to build up.

Bishops, can move any number of squares diagonally and can capture any opposing piece on a diagonal path. One of the two bishops roams dark squares, the other roams the light squares.

The queen can move any distance straight ahead, sideways or diagonally. Thus, the queen's strength lies principally in its mobility, range and omnipresence, which makes it a very potent attacking piece. Although it may be required to contribute to defence, that is not its true vocation and should be avoided. When involved in defence, the queen loses much of its mobility and, since it is too valuable piece to be sacrificed, it cannot be used as a shield for the king. Lose your queen and victory is a daunting task.

The king must, as in medieval times, be defended to the death by all the other pieces. The king, for all his stature, has limited movement, only one square at a time, albeit in any direction. Part of your ongoing game plan should be placing pieces strategically to create a defensive wall around your king.

One interesting move is "castling". This is the only situation where two pieces, always the king and the rook, move simultaneously and is only permitted if these two pieces have not already moved and the squares between the rook and the king are vacant. Castling is, quite simply, where the king moves two squares towards the rook, and the rook then hops over the king to the first square beyond it. This is often a defensive move to protect the king by moving it away from the centre of the board.

BASIC ELEMENTS OF PLAY

The game is won when the opposing king is captured or "checkmated". Whenever one player makes a move which threatens to capture the opposing king, the monarch is said to be "in check". The attacked player must take an immediate action to ward off the threat, either by moving the king away, capturing the predatory piece or interposing another piece to act as a temporary shield. If none of these defensive moves is possible and the king cannot escape capture, it is checkmate and the game is over.

In order to achieve checkmate, each king's army of pieces backed by pawns must fight each other for advancement all over the board and strive to open weaknesses in the opponent's defences, with the aim to attack the king when the moment is ripe. During the opening moves, pieces are "developed" by moving forward to occupy the most strategic positions for both attack and defence. During the middle game, the pieces are engaged in close combat and capture, leading, when the opportunity arises, to an attack on the enemy king. In the end game, with just a few pieces left on the board, the objective may be to promote a pawn to a queen which will then be able to mop up the remaining enemy pieces and apply "mate". In practice, experienced players give up (or "resign") without waiting to be mated, that is, when they realize their position has become hopeless.

As the game progresses, pieces are exchanged, with the players attempting to maintain relative equality by ensuring that, whenever a piece is lost, an enemy piece of at least equivalent value is captured.

When evaluating a game in progress, the first aspect a spectator (known as a "kibitzer") checks is whether any player has captured more pieces than the other, since the advantage of even a single pawn can often spell a win. That said, some attacking players will willingly sacrifice a pawn or even a piece (during the opening, this is known as a "gambit") to gain the initiative, open squares for other pieces or breach the opposing king's wall of defence.

The challenge in chess is combining the action of various pieces which move in different disciplines, offensively and defensively, and planning sufficiently ahead one's own moves whilst predicting and taking account of the opponent's possible replies. Such planning keeps the mind alert and functioning throughout the game and is where the intellectual pleasure of chess lies.

During a game, you are often faced with decisions to give up a piece, either to defend another or to capture a high value opposing piece. Here is an indication of the approximate value of all pieces relative to a pawn.

queen 9: rook 5: bishop 3: knight 3: pawn 1.

The king does not figure because, obviously, it can never be traded for other pieces. The queen and rook are known as "major" pieces, to be protected at all cost, whilst the bishop and knight are more "minor" in strategic value.

A word about drawn games which are frequent occurrences in top matches. Draws take place if none of one player's pieces can make a legal move and the king is not in check ("stalemate"); if there are insufficient pieces on the board to force checkmate; if the same position is repeated three times; or by mutual consent, sometimes out of fear of losing – happily not frequent amongst amateurs who have the tendency to play on where it is clearly impossible for either player to win.

These are the basics of playing chess. Going from being a novice at the game to a skilled chess player can be, for many, an absorbing passion.

Before we look at how you might go about taking up chess and learning more, let's take a brief look at some of the great players that have made a major contribution to the world of chess over the last three centuries.

SOME OF THE GAME'S GREATEST

One of the most famous chess masters during the 18th century was a Frenchman, André Philidor (1726–1795) who dominated the game for over 40 years. When only fourteen, Philidor, a musical prodigy as a child, was playing chess in the Café de la Régence in Paris against the top players in France. During his heydays, Philidor gained world celebrity by giving chess demonstrations, playing two games simultaneously, blindfolded! Philidor spent part of his chess life in London during the French Revolution.

In the 19th century, an Englishman, Howard Staunton (1810–1874) claimed his place in chess history. Born in Westmoreland, Staunton commenced his career as an actor in Shakespearean plays but took up serious chess in his mid-twenties. Over the following twenty years, he played matches against all Europe's leading players and was chess columnist for the Illustrated London News. As a tribute to his skills, in 1964, Bobby Fischer said that Staunton was the most skilled opening player of all time. A worthy epitaph for any chess master.

Paul Morphy (1837–1884), an American of Irish descent, was one of the most gifted, but eccentric, of all players in the history of chess. A recluse, given also to delusions, Morphy travelled to Paris in 1858, shortly after having become the US chess champion, and thrashed a number of top players, including the German champion Adolph Anderssen, who had won the International Chess Championship in 1851 in London. In between two of his matches, Morphy played eight simultaneous blindfold games at the Café de la Régence. During his stay in Paris, Morphy challenged the English champion, Staunton, to come over for a match but Staunton baulked and side-stepped the invitation, such were Morphy's sublime skills over the board. Morphy could have been the undisputed world champion but retired on his return to the States to live in reclusion at the pinnacle of a brilliant playing career of a scant two years, of which he spent just six months in Paris and another five months in London. He was especially admired for winning via audacious sacrifices of pieces.

José Raul Capablanca (1888–1942), born in Cuba was possibly the most talented of the all time greats in the history of chess. Having learned the rules of chess as a small boy by watching his father play, Capablanca was, by the age of thirteen, playing at the Havana Chess Club where he took on and beat all the leading players. Arriving in New York to study at Columbia University, Capablanca spent more of his time at the Manhattan Chess Club than in class. At the age of twenty, he won a match against Frank Marshall, the US champion and a few years later was playing tournament chess in Europe. At a great tournament in 1914 in Saint Petersburg, he met the awesome German chess master Emmanuel Lasker, who held the world championship for 27 years, across the chessboard for the first time. Capablanca made Lasker fight hard for a draw in their initial match and ended up second to Lasker in the overall result with the Russian Alexander Alekhine (see below) in third place. During the period 1916-1924, Capablanca was unbeaten and, during his entire chess career, suffered fewer than 50 defeats in around 600 top games. When he died in 1942, Alekhine, his great rival, wrote, "With his death, we have lost a very great chess genius whose like we shall never see again". Unlike Alekhine, Capablanca was a very relaxed player, the moves just came naturally to him.

The first world champion from Russia was Alexander Alekhine (1892-1946) with a remarkable lifestyle. Alekhine served in the Russian Red Cross in 1915-16, was a criminal investigator in Moscow in 1918, imprisoned in a death cell in Odessa a year later, got released and returned to Moscow and continued his avid pursuit of chess. In 1925, he finally emigrated to France and studied law at the Sorbonne. What a guy! That year, he was playing chess blindfolded winning twenty-two and drawing three. Alekhine was world chess champion 1927–1946, except 1935 to 1937.

Mikhail Botvinnik (1911–1995), another Russian from Saint Petersburg took over the reins from Alekhine and was world champion 1948–1960 and 1963. Botvinnik had a PhD in Electrical Engineering and worked on computer chess programming. It is of note that C.H.O'D. Alexander, twice British chess champion and member of Alan Turing's Enigma code-breaking team at Bletchley Park in 1939–42, beat Botvinnik in an Anglo-Soviet match in 1946. Alexander was one of these rare breeds of top chess players, a highly talented amateur who played against professionals in his leisure time.

Enter Bobby Fischer

In an encounter that was called the chess match of the century and which took place in Iceland, the reigning world champion, Boris Spassky, another Russian, was beaten by Bobby Fischer of the US in 1972.

Today's world of chess abounds with tales of the enigmatic Bobby Fischer's achievements and continued speculation and news about his whereabouts and playing activities that sporadically hit the headlines oddly reminiscent of that other fellow American, Paul Morphy.

Fischer is a man of exceptional intelligence, with an IQ of around 180 and a prodigious memory. It is said that he has such an incredible memory that he can recall most of the moves made in speed chess games (discussed later) he has played, when both players are limited to sometimes as few as three minutes to make all their moves. For example, after the World Speed Chess Championship in Yugoslavia in 1970, legend has it that he rattled off from memory the scores of all his twenty-two games, involving more than a thousand moves.

After defeating Spassky in 1972, Bobby Fischer, curiously, at the height of his playing career, withdrew from competition and was stripped of his world title by the FIDE, the World Chess Federation, in 1975.

After the loss of his world chess title in 1975, Fischer disappeared from the scene, re-emerging only once, in 1992, to play in Yugoslavia in a twenty years anniversary rematch with Spassky, which he won. He again withdrew from the limelight, taking with him the prize of five million dollars. Since that date, Fischer has been on the run from the US authorities who accuse him of breaking UN sanctions by playing professionally in Serbia.

In 2004, British grandmaster Nigel Short, who in 1993 unsuccessfully challenged the Russian Garry Kasparov for the world title, announced publicly that he had been playing speed chess on the internet and strongly suspected that his opponent was none other than Bobby Fischer, the modern, and equally elusive, Scarlet Pimpernel of chess.

Short, who is a world-class speed chess player and who drew a series of speed chess games with

Garry Kasparov in 1995, reported that he had lost all matches of a fascinating series against his anonymous opponent.

In some online chat, Short, eager to coax his formidable opponent into revealing his identity, asked if he (or she) knew of an obscure Mexican tournament player, giving the name. Immediately, back came the response, yes, in Siegen 1970. Bobby Fischer played against the name given by Short at the Siegen Chess Olympiad in 1970!

It remains to be seen if Nigel Short's mystery opponent will resume the online combat now that the cat may be out of the bag. Whatever the sequel, Nigel Short's comment in his statement to the press was eloquent testimony to Bobby Fischer's status in world chess: "To me, these games are what an undiscovered Mozart symphony would be to a music lover".

Kasparov, another all time great.

Garry Kasparov was a protégé of the great Mikhail Botvinnik, who declared that "the future of chess lies in the hands of this young man" when Kasparov was aged eleven. Wise words, since Kasparov is today widely considered as one of the greatest players in the history of world chess.

In 1982, Kasparov took on the reigning world champion Anatoly Karpov in a marathon, 48 game event, lasting five months. Both players were so exhausted, particularly Karpov, twelve years older, that the FIDE, the World Chess Federation, declared the event a draw and Karpov retained his title. The following year, the match was replayed and Kasparov beat Karpov to win his first World Championship, a title he held until the mid–1990s. Kasparov retired from chess in 2005, just after losing his last competitive game against Veselin

Topalov, from Bulgaria and winner of the FIDE World
Chess Championship in 2005.

MAN VERSUS MACHINE MATCHES

No introduction to the world of chess would be complete
without mention of the role now played by computers.

A decade ago, IBM developed Deep Blue, a chess
application–specific mainframe computer designed
to compete against the grandmasters. In 1997, Garry
Kasparov played a series of six games against Deep
Blue.

Deep Blue was a 1.4 ton RS/6000 computer, programmed
by a five-man IBM team of top technicians, expert in
chess software, with an international grandmaster, Joel
Benjamin, as consultant, and was equipped with a total
of 256 processors working in parallel. Deep Blue at
the time was capable of calculating 200 million chess
positions per second. Its downside was that it could not
"think" like a human brain and evaluate its opponent's
positioning weaknesses and thus capitalize on these
to adapt its playing strategy. Any changes in the way
it played had to be made by programmers in between
games.

Garry Kasparov, at that time aged 34, had been
world chess champion since 1985. He is estimated to be
capable of evaluating three chess positions per second,
with an ability to switch tactics with incredible dexterity
to outwit his opponent. His downside is that like all
human beings, and unlike a computer, he is liable to the
hazards of fatigue and loss of concentration under stress
conditions.

The results of the 1997 event were: first game to
Kasparov, second game, one month later, to Deep Blue,
then a sequence of one game to each and a draw over

the next three months ...and the final, and decisive battle was won by Deep Blue, making the overall result Deep Blue the winner with three games to two for Garry Kasparov and one drawn.

Deep Fritz is another computer chess machine which has recently hit the headlines in matches against top players. Developed by two German programmers, Deep Fritz took on the Russian grandmaster Vladimir Kramnik in 2002 in an eight-game match in Bahrain, which ended in a draw.

After five games with wins by both sides, game six was described by tournament commentators as "spectacular". Kramnik, in a better position than Fritz in the early middle game, tried to sacrifice a piece to achieve a strong tactical attack, a strategy known to be fraught with risk against computers which tend to be at their strongest defending such moves. True to form, Fritz found a watertight defence and Kramnik's attack petered out. Believing the position hopeless, Kramnik resigned. A post-game man and computer analysis concluded that it is unlikely that the Fritz programme would have been able to force a win and Kramnik had effectively sacrificed a drawn result. Although the overall result of the match was a draw, most commentators still rate Kramnik the stronger player in that duel of man versus computer.

HOW TO GET STARTED IN CHESS

So, to leave the giddy heights of chess geniuses matching skills against blinking computers and get back to real life. What is the best way to start to find out if you can get interested in taking up chess as an absorbing pastime?

The vast majority of players have picked up the basics of the game informally at home or with friends, sometimes just from watching others play (nothing informal about learning chess in the ex-Soviet Union where it was virtually compulsory to play at the party youth association – no wonder they dominate the winner's podium at international chess tournaments).

Obviously, the essential starting point is to learn how the pieces move, capturing, castling, promotion of pawns and, of course, the positioning for checkmate. After this initial step, the more often you play, the quicker you progress. Ideally, you should try to find an experienced player (the patient friend) who accepts to invest the time and patience to coach a beginner.

The next stage would be to join a club, if at all possible. Most clubs offer tuition, ideally to those who have already picked up the rudiments of the game. Unlike bridge, coaching is appropriate at all stages of the learning curve of chess, and even later for strong and experienced players.

If you are not fortunate to have any playing contacts and you live in a remote area, as for all the pastimes discussed in this book, there are many websites available to provide guidance on chess rules and playing tactics.

Here are a couple of excellent websites which I believe would be helpful to someone interested in taking up the game and wanting to have a closer insight.

- www.chessvariants.com, edited by Hans Bodlaender of The Netherlands, who is a senior lecturer in computer sciences at Utrecht University, with a team of other editors. Bodlaender teaches chess to youngsters
- www.chess.about.com, edited by Mark Weeks, who is a graduate of Cornell University, and is now living in Europe. Has a high FIDE rating and works as a corporate international IT project manager. A great website that takes you through the game nice and easy.

If you do not have access to the Web, you could visit your local bookstore or library and select one of hundreds of books now available on chess.

One bestseller about learning to play is *Bobby Fischer Teaches Chess* by...Bobby Fischer!

Here are a couple of other suggestions:

Chess for Beginners
    by D B Pritchard
Starting Out in Chess
    by Byron Jacobs

LEARNING MORE

Here is a further dimension to playing chess, which could be useful as you expand your knowledge of the finer points of the game.

Chess notation

For anyone interested in taking up chess seriously, reading accounts of famous games is one way to advance one's skills. Some newspapers have a daily chess column which give readers a move-by-move "score" of great games, containing diagrams and annotations. One such newspaper is The Times with a column by Raymond Keene. This column is also available online at www. timesonline.co.uk.

As an example, one game that appeared in The Times chess column when I was writing this chapter was a match at the British Empire Club Masters in London in 1927 between Aron Nimzowitsch, a Latvian chess master, and William Winter, British Chess Champion in 1935 and 1936. Winter was a colourful character, being the nephew of Sir James Barrie, the creator of Peter Pan, and was chess journalist for the Manchester Guardian and the Daily Worker (an interesting indication that all classes of society played chess in the early 1900s). He pursued a radical political career and gained somewhat dubious celebrity in the chess world for being the only chess master to be imprisoned for sedition!

How are such games reported in the newspaper? The answer to that question is by using what is called "chess notation". At this point I would stress that you can take up and enjoy chess perfectly well without knowing anything about chess notation but it is an added plus to your learning curve.

Here is a brief outline of algebraic chess notation. If the word "algebraic" is a bit intimidating to those who are non-maths minded, have no fear, it is said that lots of seven-year olds can master the technique easily, although, to be fair, nothing is said about seventy-year olds.

The chessboard has 8x8 squares, making 64 squares in total. Each of the eight columns of squares going up and down the board is called a "file". Files are denoted with small letters a,b,c,d,e,f,g,h. Note that the "a" file is always on the white player's left and on the black player's right.

Each of the eight lines of squares running in horizontal lines across the board is called a "rank" and are numbered 1,2,3,4,5,6,7 and 8. White starts from ranks 1&2, Black commences on ranks 8&7.

Each piece has a capital letter representing its name. The king=K; queen=Q; rook=R; knight=N; bishop=B. No letters are used for the pawns.

Thus, the board, with its algebraic notations, looks like this at the start of a game.

	a	b	c	d	e	f	g	h	
8	R	N	B	Q	K	B	N	R	8 (Black pieces)
7	p	p	p	p	p	p	p	p	7
6									6
5									5
4									4
3									3
2	p	p	p	p	p	p	p	p	2
1	R	N	B	Q	K	B	N	R	1 (White pieces)
	a	b	c	d	e	f	g	h	

A move of any piece is annotated by the letter of the moving piece followed by the address of the square to which it is moved. Moves by pawns are noted by only the destination square address. A capture by a piece is indicated by the capturing piece name, followed by an "x", and then the capture square address.

For the sake of illustration of how the system works, in the Nimzowitsch/ Winter game, here are the first and second moves by both players, followed by their 19th move, as an example of notation of a capture.

1b3 e5 2Bb2 f6......and 19Bxd5 Rb8

The first two opening moves were: Nimzowitsch (playing white) moves a pawn forward one step to square b3 (note, not the permitted two-steps starter). Winter (playing black) responds by moving a pawn two steps forward to square e5. Now, second move. White moves his bishop diagonally left one space to b2 (vacated by his first pawn move) to b2, move noted as Bb2. Black follows by moving his f pawn one step to square f6.

In move 19 (Bxd5) the "x" indicates a capture, with White moving his bishop to d5 to capture a pawn. Black responds by moving his rook to b8 noted as Rb8.

The score contained 45 moves apiece by the two adversaries until White "resigned".

Learning from historic chess match reports

Here is an outline of how a beginner can learn from studying a daily newspaper chess column giving reports of chess games between top players.

First, try to obtain a chessboard with notations already printed along the sides. I am fortunate to have such a board, on loan from a friend who inherited it from his grandfather, which dates it back to the 19th century. If an annotated board is not easily found, paste the 1–8 and a-h notations on the edges of a normal chessboard. Then, place the black and white pieces in their starting positions on the board. You are now ready to re-enact a game played, possibly between two opposing chess grandmasters!

Now select a chess game report and commence to move the pieces, white first, followed by black, as indicated by the report. After the first few moves, pause and contemplate which move you might make if you were playing white, either to attack or defend a vulnerable piece, and simultaneously what move black might make either in response or in the form of an offensive game plan. Then refer to the game report and see what move white actually made and how black responded and move the pieces accordingly.

Continue throughout the game this process of advance contemplation of moves by white and responses by black and comparison with what took place and keep score of how many times play proceeded as you would have planned. Make notes on some of the more intriguing opening moves as part of your learning process. Above all, try to place yourself in the mindset of the players, it's a great way to learn!

CORRESPONDENCE CHESS

If you live in a remote area and cannot find opponents, correspondence (or postal) chess is an enjoyable pastime to play against an enthusiast whom you may never meet face to face. Correspondence chess, as the name implies, is played by writing your move by notation on a card, mailing it to your opponent and waiting for a reply counter move. Virtually everything is allowed except you are honour bound not to consult other players. A postal game can last anywhere between six and eighteen months within your own postal system, much longer if you are playing against a Russian (who are great fans of correspondence chess) since the Russian postal system is even worse than in western Europe. Given the long intervals between moves, some enthusiasts play correspondence chess against multiple opponents.

Correspondence chess is not new, having been played since the early 19th century. In 1824 it is on record that the London Chess Club challenged the Edinburgh Chess Club to a correspondence match. The letters were carried four hundred miles by mail coach and delivered within three days: probably better than today's mail! The match involved the best out of three decisive games and took four years to complete.

Another interesting anecdote about postal chess is that the actor Humphrey Bogart was visited by FBI agents in 1943, alleging that his chess notations to correspondents overseas were secret enemy codes. Sounds like one of Bogart's movies!

Inevitably, with the advent of the internet, correspondence chess now incorporates the possibility of playing chess games using e-mail which changes the pace of communication completely.

To learn more, the Scottish Correspondence Chess Association (SCCA), launched in 1998, has a splendid website, www.scottishcca.co.uk, which contains a section How to Play Correspondence Chess, including all about chess by e-mail, and also gives a list of members and players with contact addresses. Another contact for more information is the British Federation for Correspondence Chess (BFCC). Consult its website at www.bfcc-online. org.uk

BLITZ OR SPEED CHESS

Although, as a beginner to chess, it may be a long time, if ever, before you play blitz chess, it might be interesting at this point to know more about this type of play since it can be an excellent spectator pastime.

Most club games, and all tournaments, are played with chess clocks. These are composed of two interconnected clocks, one for each player, which record the thinking time between each move. As soon as a player has made his move, he presses a lever which stops his clock and automatically activates that of his opponent. The total times per game to complete all moves is set in advance and can be, say, an hour, or thirty minutes, or even as little as three minutes for each player to complete all his moves.

The purpose of chess clocks is to prevent any player gaining an unfair advantage by spending an unreasonably long time over each move since this can be highly disconcerting for a more mentally agile and decisive opponent. It also forces players to think fast, especially when time is running out, a situation which is called "zeitnot". A game in which both players are in zeitnot can be terrifically exciting to watch, with spectators crowding around the board, as each player bangs his piece down and whacks the clock lever and anxiously glances at his clock to see the remaining available time. The game is over when either one player has exhausted his time limit before his opponent, or is checkmate. Easy for a Kasparov who sizes up three deft moves per second but pretty hectic for normal mortals.

AND SEE THE MOVIE...

Finally, there is one film which is a must for all lovers of chess and which I found wonderful viewing. The film, Searching for Bobby Fischer, is based on the real life boyhood experience of a chess enthusiast, Josh Waitzkin who is now in his early twenties, plays professional chess and also teaches chess in Manhattan. The film tells us of how Josh as a six-year old became fascinated by the outdoor chess games in New York's Washington Square Park and subsequently devotes his whole youth entirely to excellence in chess.

Watch great scenes where Josh, as a youngster, is playing, and winning speed chess games, complete with the clunking of chess clocks to time swift and decisive moves, against hardened pros in the park. The movie has also old newsreels, flashbacks in black and white of Bobby Fischer in his heyday. In real life, Waitzkin, when he was eleven, as part of a group of fifty-seven kids playing simultaneously, pitted his wits against Kasparov and managed a drawn game.

A final thought. If you can make a trip to New York, and want to see real action, a visit to Washington Square Park would be a great baptism to the wonderful world of chess.

CHAPTER 5

Surfing The Web

AN INTRODUCTION TO PERSONAL COMPUTING

First, allow me to preface this chapter with a caveat since it is an introduction to personal computing, written for, what a Dutch lady friend of mine terms, "virgins on the web"! If, as is quite possible, you, like many people, have already lost your digital virginity, I hope that there may be some comments that will provide ideas to expand your pleasure of computing.

First, for newcomers to computing, here are a few comments about personal computers (PCs), which would be your access tool to the internet for what is popularly known as surfing the web. You have a choice of two types of PCs.

One option, requiring a fair amount of space and not easily moved around, is a desktop computer. A "desktop" consists of a computer "box", the processor linked to a screen, also called a monitor, and a keyboard and "mouse" to operate. A mouse, by the way, is a command mechanism to send instructions, using a finger, to the computer in tandem with the keyboard. It may sound a bit complicated at first but operating a mouse is really easy.

Your second option is a portable PC, also called a laptop or notebook. Much more compact than a desktop, a portable has the advantage that it is an all-in-one lightweight computer that you can travel with, in a bag slung over the shoulder. A portable can also operate on rechargeable batteries for a limited period of time so that you can operate when away from a mains power source. More and more, you see people on trains and planes working away on their portable. Expensive? A bit more pricey than a basic desktop but due to the ever-increasing market demand and advancing technology, prices of portables are competitive. Shop around before buying, including support for some tuition on how to operate.

One last piece of equipment for which you may well want to opt for is a printer. This will enable you to run off copies, on normal A4-sized paper, of any text or pictures held on file in the computer. The different types of printer which you might want to consider, depending on your needs, are discussed later.

WHY BUY A PC?

How many times do you hear, "me, buy a PC, what on earth would I use one for?" One general answer to that is that PCs represent an advanced piece of communication equipment used by millions of people, not just by businesses but also in homes worldwide. This chapter will outline some of the reasons why PCs are now an integral part of life for so many people.

A recognized authority on the subject, Nielsen// NetRatings reported, at the end of 2004, that around 100 million Europeans now have computer skills to surf the web, an increase of twelve per cent over the preceding year. By major country, the increases in one year were Germany (12%), UK (13%), Italy (15%) and France (16%). In contrast, Switzerland rose only 5%, Spain 3% and Sweden a paltry 1%!

In Britain alone, Nielsen//NetRatings estimated that,

by the end of 2004, there were 23 million people surfing the web, a figure skewed mainly towards the younger generation. One study in 2005 reckoned that, although 75% of 11–34 year-olds are now regular internet users, the proportion falls to around only 13% of those who are 65 and over. So, why not you, if you are not already active in this new digital age?

Another answer to the question of why take up computing is that learning to master the art of PCs is a wonderful way of keeping one's mind active and inquisitive by being in touch with the outside world and being occupied intelligently.

WHAT YOU CAN DO WITH A PC

Surfing the web is when you are connecting with internet websites to get all sorts of information to know more, using the web as a source of world news, or getting things done more efficiently.

The internet is an all-in-one shop window at your fingertips that replaces those long treks around the market place to research the best products, quality versus price, before buying, providing today's purchasing power for the consumer.

It is also a vast, continually updated, source of knowledge. All you have to do is enter two to three words of your need to know more into a website called a search engine and, seconds later, you have on your screen references to sources of study from, not just your own country, but worldwide.

A PC also enables you to:

- send written messages and pictures via the internet in the form of e-mail. E-mail is a means to establish more frequent contact with old friends and family and has the distinct advantage over "snail mail" in that e-mail arrives within seconds of being sent, anywhere in the world.

- write and store text, a "must" if you are a prolific writer. Writing using a PC enables you to make changes to text easily without recourse to an eraser and/or the frustrating scrapping of pages and rewriting, inherent with handwritten works. You can also transfer files of text and images on to CD (compact disk) or, even better, a "pen drive" for more permanent storage. A pen drive, about the size and shape of a man's forefinger, can store massive amounts of data for easy retrieval or retransfer to your computer.

- record music, now legally possible using the internet. A wide selection of classical and popular music is available for free listening, and for recording on a CD, at a cost of much less than buying the recording in the market.

- process digital photos. The huge popularity of the digital camera can be a prime motivation for buying a PC to process, archive and present your own digital photos on screen, and transmit photos to friends by e-mail. This can be an engrossing PC pastime in itself and can also be a stepping stone to your becoming familiar with the basics of operating a computer, and gaining the necessary confidence to expand into many of the other applications outlined in this chapter. Much more about processing digital photos in chapter 8, Going Digital.

Later in this chapter, you will find more precision about the main uses of a PC. But, first, a few words about how the web came to be developed.

THE ORIGINS OF THE WEB

The world wide web, or simply www, was the brainchild of a British-born computer scientist, Timothy J. Berners-Lee, back in 1980 while working at CERN, the Centre Européen pour la Recherche Nucléaire, based near Geneva. His mandate was to instigate more systematic sharing of research information throughout the vast organization. He and his team achieved this by creating a network linking the data held on computer files of some 5,000 CERN researchers. In other words, sharing information through computers talking to computers. So, the origins of the web were yet another case of necessity being the mother of invention.

By 1991, Berners-Lee and his team had extended this successful internal project of connectivity at CERN to create a global network, or what is now called the internet, using a vast web of computers to disseminate published and commercial information worldwide.

This information is presented by way of websites designed and inserted in the internet by manufacturing companies, product distributors, historians, universities and academics, scientists, campaigners, foundations, governments, and people of all tastes and intelligence, in short, anybody who wants to publish information to the world at large. Note that the web does not enable unauthorized access to confidential or classified data such as banks, social security, tax records and so on.

Of course, there is also a lot of frivolous and "adult" stuff on the web. Let me say just this: think of the web as being similar in content quality to your broad range of national newspapers and weekly magazines, catering to all tastes in a highly diversified society. With newspapers, you have, in Britain, the likes of the Daily Telegraph and the Guardian at the upper end of the spectrum and the popular press at the other with content that is often fact mixed with fancy to appeal to their readers. And you have magazines like The Economist and The New Scientist with serious content and, at the other, more popular end of the market, a wide variety of magazines, including crime, sex and scandal. Like all those publications, the web has a highly diversified content, including sex which often gives the internet a totally unjustified bad name since those uninterested in porn need never be aware of its existence on the web. The web has also video features and games and online popular music, all particularly favoured by the younger generation.

So, when surfing the web, the choice of on which wave to head the surfboard is entirely up to the surfer!

SURFING THE WEB

Accessing a website is achieved by linking your PC to an internet service provider (ISP), which are mostly large telephone companies, via your home telephone line. Your dealer will pre-programme your PC to dial into the ISP number for access to the web.

It should be mentioned at this point that, whilst the internet can be accessed by a normal home telephone line, this can take up a lot of online time in transmission of data.

All ISPs offer subscribers, for a modest monthly fee, broadband, which is a fibre optics line (as opposed to the old lines made of copper wire), also called DSL, which stands for Digital Subscriber Line. With broadband, access to the web and transmission of text and images by e-mail is perhaps ten times quicker and therefore reduces online time and cost. A dash for broadband around Europe over the last two years has now resulted in extensive coverage in most countries, mostly due to competitive selling by the internet providers. It is predicted that in Britain alone eight million households will be equipped with DSL by 2008.

Making contact with the web is called "logging on". You can log on to a website and search for and locate all kinds of information, within minutes, a task which previously would have taken days or even weeks via books, magazines, enquiries of friends and business contacts or extensive visits to department stores, shops, or government departments.

Accessing the internet with a mobile phone

Many mobile phone operators offer a contract for accessing the web by mobile phone for a monthly fee. For this, you require a mobile handset equipped with a modem (for the technically minded, a modem converts analogue data to digital for transmission over a fixed telephone line or by radio). You also require a cable linking your mobile handset to your PC. Your vendor will programme your PC to call up the number of your ISP via your mobile. Then all you have to do is log on to your ISP's website, via your PC linked to your mobile phone, in exactly the same way as with a fixed telephone line. Using a mobile phone to access the web is an ideal arrangement for being away from home and not having easy access to a normal fixed telephone.

Search engines

As previously noted, these are websites specially designed to seek out other websites which contain information on almost any subject which you, the user, want to know more about. There is now a wide choice of search engines, which include (in order of popularity in the UK); Google, Yahoo, Alta Vista, Tiscali, My Way and MSN.

WHAT THE WEB CAN DO FOR YOU

Since everybody has a different lifestyle, here are a few random examples of areas of activity that might be of interest to some readers.

- Staying informed, with news that interests you
- Travel: by low cost airlines, and by road to a new foreign destination
- Shopping: the web is now a giant department store and provides access to product distributors
- Show business: perhaps to know more about a performer you have heard on the radio or seen on TV
- Health: learn more about implications of some medical treatment
- Pastimes: getting information to fuel your pastime in life
- Finding out more about the world around us.

Let's look at examples of each of these applications.

Staying informed

If, say, you are planning an evening out with friends, and you will miss the evening news on television or radio, all you have to do log on to www.bbc.co.uk, a splendid website also known as bbcnews.com, updated as news breaks, by the BBC worldwide team of journalists. This is a great way of staying informed at any time of the day about items of news and subjects that interest you.

The BBC website contains both written and audio reports on national and international news at a glance, with detailed news by world regions, linked to previous reports on the same subject, business news, world stock markets on a real time basis, individual stock prices and currency rates, weather forecasts, where you live and worldwide, for your travel, for the next five days, all the sports news, home and international, with profiles of the big hitters, new developments of interest on the health scene, reports on technology, science/nature, and highlights on show business, art, cinema and more.

With a website like the BBC's, you can be selective. It is so much more efficient.

And that's not all. The BBC website has also a search engine. If you have a subject that you want to know more about, all you have to do is key in two or three words of description and the site will throw up perhaps pages of reports on the subject, going back in time, as prepared by their team of 5,000 journalists around the globe, with references to other websites, giving you in-depth and serious research at your fingertips. If you want hard copy for further analysis, run off copies on your printer and put on file.

I am far from being alone in preferring the free access BBC website to reading a newspaper for my daily update on world news, business and markets, science/nature and technology. The Economist recently reported that the BBC site's audience has increased from 1.6 million unique weekly users in 2000 to 7.8 million in 2005. And total newspaper circulation has fallen by around 30% since 1990 and continues to falter.

Another means of using your PC to get news is to log on to any of the websites offered by the newspapers or weekly news magazines in many countries. Log on to a search engine for the website address of the newspaper or magazine of your choice. In Britain, for example, most of the national newspapers have websites which are a reproduction of the paper which you buy at a kiosk. Log on to, say, www.timesonline.co.uk and you will find that same day's copy of either The Times or the Sunday Times with headline news from around the world and reports in detail on all of your interests. And this can be done either from home or on your portable PC anywhere in the world if you are travelling or on holiday. Access to most of these websites is free (apart from the cost of the telephone line) except some papers, such as the Financial Times, that request a paid subscription for certain in-depth reports. Not surprising that newspaper sales are dropping, such is the way that the internet is changing our daily lives.

Travel: Booking trips by air

If you are planning a holiday by air and are flexible about dates, preferring best value, booking a flight via the web enables you to surf most airlines' computers and check out on what dates and flights their planes are running at under-capacity and therefore, to fill seats, tickets are low cost. You don't always get this kind of favourable deal from a travel agent and low cost airlines do not work with travel agents so DIY (do-it-yourself) booking is no longer an option but a necessity.

You can also see pictures of your destination on other websites, and check out hotel accommodation for competitive pricing and choice without relying on a travel agent.

Travel: Mapping road trips for foreign destinations

Supposing you plan to drive from your home base in England to Chamonix, nestling at the foot of Mont Blanc in the French Alps, taking the cross-Channel ferry to

Calais. From Calais, you would like more precision on the best choice of route.

Log-on to www.viamichelin.com, a website provided on a free basis by the Michelin tyre company for promotion of its products, and key in Calais to Chamonix in the spaces provided. The website, which is pan-European, will, within seconds, provide you with a detailed itinerary via Reims, in champagne country.

Plan a stop-over near Reims by "clicking", that is, using the mouse, on the space " book online", and you are switched on to an annexed website where you are able to reserve a room at the four-star Grand Hôtel de Templiers in Reims. Then on to Besançon and finally into the Alpes to your destination. The website tells you the distance between towns along the route, with estimated travel times and even how much cash you should plan to have for motorway tolls. All you have to do now is print out the itinerary, stow it away in the car glove compartment and you're off.

Shopping

Another illustration of the Web's versatility to the user is shopping from home. If you are a keen reader and cannot make a trip to one of these superb inner city bookstores, you can buy books online. All you have to do is access a major bookstore website such as Amazon or WHSmith. Browsing on the online book website, you can select your favourite authors or book titles you wish to consider. Or select a subject in which you are interested and the site will give you lists of books, with author's name and price, from which you can take your pick. Once your order is complete, you pay by giving your credit card details, key in your mailing address and your books, within days, will be delivered by post.

If you are thinking of buying a new car, save yourself the hassle of often long sales pitches by salesmen, eager to clinch a sale. With the internet, you can now, in advance of the visit to a dealer, log on to the websites of the main distributors where you will find illustrated information on each model and options, with technical data and pricing. Once prepared, you can then visit a selection of car showrooms to negotiate the purchase of exactly what fits your needs, on your terms, and trade in your old model.

A formidable boost to consumer power has been online browsing to get the best prices through price comparison sites. If you live in Britain, a website such as www.paler.com/price_comparison.html provides a guide to about twenty UK price comparison sites which you can surf to research the best buys for a wide range of consumer goods such as household appliances, DVDs, CDs, jewellery, travel offers, digital cameras, camcorders, cosmetics, clothing and lots more.

How does a price comparison site work? If you wanted to buy, as an example, eau de toilette at the best possible price, a website such as www.uk.shopping.com (selected from the above twenty UK price comparison sites) provides a range of offers for health and beauty products, including eau de toilette, plus offers of many other goods such as refrigerators, ovens, clothing, computers, mobile phones and so on. Focus on the "fragrances" section of the site and you find a selection of fragrances (eau de toilette, colognes, perfumes etc), plus two other columns, price ranges and brands. Select "eau de toilette" and your chosen price range and out comes a page of offers of different brands with prices in your range. If you were to choose, say, Chanel as your preferred brand, a switch to that name in the site will throw up on the screen the line of Chanel eau de toilettes in your price range. You are also given a choice of seven to eight online shopping sources with comparative prices for each product. All done in a few minutes at home. You can either order online or, if you prefer, have an outing to the shops, and breathe the fragrance before buying, with market prices in mind to get the best buy. Price comparison sites are yet another example of the new style shopping intelligence available from the internet.

Same routine for that new laptop! Open up the section "computers" and select the price range of £560–£720 for portables. There you have spread out before you models from IBM, H-P, Acer, Toshiba and Fujitsu Siemens. Compare the prices and consider a direct buy versus a visit to your local dealers for a price-negotiated deal that includes start-up tuition.

Show business

Say you hear a really good song on the radio and you would like to know more about the singer and what CDs are available. Take, for example, songs by the global artist, songwriter and singer Chris de Burgh. All you have to do is log on to a search engine and key in the words "Chris de Burgh" in the space provided. Within seconds, you will have on your screen, pages of lists of pertinent websites which you can open up and learn that he was born in Argentina, of British parents. Through his father's career, Chris lived in various countries in Central Africa before finally settling down in Ireland, where he studied at Trinity College, Dublin and gained a degree in French and English. His remarkable career dates back to 1975, when his debut single "Flying" hit the No. 1 spot in Brazil. He has since won over 200 gold and platinum awards. His evergreen classic, "Lady in Red" has sold over eight million copies worldwide and his fans included Diana, Princess of Wales, Boris Yeltsin and Helmut Kohl. The websites contain information on all his albums which you can order online.

Health questions

If someone dear to you is facing, say, a kidney transplant, and you want to know more about the subject, access a search engine and key in "kidney transplant". Within seconds, the engine will indicate a large number of pages of websites, one of which is, for example, produced by the NHS called "kidneytransplantguide.org.uk" which does just what its title says.

Leisure activities

Other examples of where a search engine produces outstanding results are for many of the leisure activities set out in other chapters of this book. Take, for example, genealogy which requires extensive research of external sources of information such as public archives, now available through the internet. Better to avoid the expense of a visit in person to a far-off location if you can identify in advance information available via the web to ensure that a journey would not be a waste of time.

For those interested in the ever-changing facets of the environment, the BBC's website with its section Science/Nature not only provides a daily update of news on climate change and how it is damaging our planet but it allows you to go back to past reports to assist your learning curve of the key issue at stake.

The BBC's website Science/Nature also covers the latest developments in man's exploration of outer space and the science of astronomy. The section provides loads of knowledge about astronomy via past reports and sites hosted by Sir Patrick Moore, the BBC's spaceman extraordinary. In pursuit of my interest in astronomy, I wanted an update on the latest news from a spacecraft, the Cassini-Huygens orbiting one of Saturn's moons called Titan, where there is much speculation of possible extraterrestrial life. I logged on to the European Space Agency's website, www.esa.int and was able to scan the reports on observations and images relayed from Huygens millions of miles away in outer space.

If you were to be contemplating a visit to an archaeological site in, say, Greece and first want to know more about its background history, all you have to do is log on to Google or Yahoo and key in the name of the site. And if you would like to examine options to plan a visit to Greece, key in, say, Archaeology tours Greece and you will be greeted with literally thousands of sites to access information on organized tours to visit famous sites such as Athens, Delphi, Mycenae, Olympia, Epidaurus and many more.

Finding out more

Finally, the internet is a great source to know more about many questions that arise in day-to-day life. For example, when I was writing about desalination for the chapter 6, Protecting the Planet, I asked myself, fine, we all know that the sea is saltwater, but why? Logging on to the BBC website mentioned above, I keyed in " why seawater salty" and was rewarded by many mentions of the subject, notably in sites headed GCSE SOS Teacher, aimed, of course, at schoolchildren (and retired people, like me, who have forgotten what they learned in school). Here is a summary of what some of the reports in the site explained re why seawater contains salt.

The main source of the planet's fresh water is, of course, rainfall. The heat of the sun on the oceans results in evaporation as pure unsalted water. The vapour rises skywards, forms clouds which then precipitate, that is, the vapour is condensed into drops and falls as rain. As the rainwater percolates through soil and rocks, it absorbs salt and duly flows into lakes and rivers and eventually to the sea. Note, however, that this only constitutes a negligible fraction of seawater salinity today, the saline content being a build-up since the planet was formed billions of years ago.

The BBC site also revealed that other reasons for seawater salinity may be submarine volcanic eruptions, and also "hydrothermal vents", only recently discovered, but did not elaborate. Switching to other websites via Google, I learned that, in 1977, a US Navy, three-man submarine, called Alvin and specially conceived for deep sea dives, discovered, off the coast of Ecuador at a depth of 2.5 kilometres, super hot (380°C) vents on the ocean floor. These vents, now called "smokers", spew out dark plumes of minerals from the Earth's crust. Scientists are now studying the possibility that hydrothermal vents have contributed to the salinity of the sea over the past billions of years.

Another excellent source for almost all the need-to-know information that one could possibly imagine is the world's first online encyclopaedia, Wikipedia.

Wikipedia was founded in 2001 by an independently wealthy entrepreneur, Jimmy Wales, as a non-profit, multi-lingual database of information for free access by people worldwide. Wales, now head of Wikipedia Foundation, based in St Petersburg in Florida, the body which owns the encyclopaedia, works unpaid with a very small staff. Wikipedia is now available, in order of volume of content, in English, German, French, Polish, Dutch, Italian and Spanish.

In fact, the website content of what are termed "articles"

is not compiled internally but by large numbers of outside volunteer writers of multiple nationalities from all walks of life with widely varying knowledge skills. Not only that but anyone can edit, delete or replace an article. Which by the very definition puts Wikipedia's reliability on the line. According, however, to a recent report by the respected scientific journal, Nature, whilst some isolated inserts to this online encyclopaedia may contain errors in scientific articles, on the whole Wikipedia is no more unreliable in the area of science than the venerable Encyclopaedia Britannica. Not surprisingly, the scholarly encyclopaedia protested about this claim that the online upstart could match its accuracy. The jury is still out on this one.

As a random example of what you can do with this online encyclopaedia, I had occasion to look up the article on the life and works of John Buchan, the well known Scottish writer and politician who was, at the height of his career as a statesman, Baron Tweedsmuir, a title bestowed on him by King George VI when he became Governor General of Canada in 1935 until his death in 1940.

Logging on to www.wikipedia.org and keying in his name, the five pages of his biography indicated that Buchan was not only a great writer but also had an interesting professional career, first as a journalist for The Times and officer in intelligence during WW1 after studies at Glasgow University and Oxford, then as Director of Information after the war and later he was an elected Scottish Unionist MP. He was a prolific writer, including a number of biographies such as those of Sir Walter Scott and Oliver Cromwell, but he is best known for his Richard Hannay spy thriller novels, notably the Thirty-Nine Steps (made into a film by Alfred Hitchcock) and Greenmantle.

One very useful aspect of most of Wikipedia's articles is that they provide links to other external websites for supplementary information creating a veritable web of intelligence for the reader.

To conclude these examples of what you can find on the web, I see this as a more proactive approach to self-education than spending time watching often futile television news and programmes in the hope that your needs for information turn up.

It may be that, like countless others, you will discover that, over time, surfing the web will develop into an engrossing and fruitful activity.

Digging for knowledge can generate interests and enjoyment in all sorts of related fields. As the French say, "l'appétit vient en mangeant", appetite comes when eating!

CHEAP TELEPHONE CALLS BY…VOIP

A new exciting technology is now on the market and goes by the name of VOIP (Voice Over Internet Protocol). One pioneer of VOIP is a company called Skype. Skype provides a service that enables users to make long distance phone calls, worldwide, using a PC linked to the internet over broadband, which means calls at cheap internet connection rates. The trick is to equip your PC with Skype software and a headset, or a handset linked to what is called the USB port on your PC, and you are set up for voice communication like a normal telephone call.

Phone calls to correspondents similarly geared up at the other end with Skype software are free because of the use of internet. Not only are the calls free but Skype-to-Skype calls cannot be listened in to by outsiders since the voice transmission is "scrambled" using encryption technology but providing normal speak between caller and correspondent. Seems like a boon for the international criminal fraternity but this is standard to the system for all users, with no extra charge.

Even if you have someone you want to call long distance who is not equipped with Skype, say, to family or friends, you can make the calls to them with your PC/ Skype, at rates roughly equivalent to a local call or free if you have the broadband contract on a fixed monthly fee mentioned above.

VOIP is catching on fast between persons or companies on different continents who are in regular contact by phone. There are mothers in India who are calling their computer whiz-kid sons in California's Silicon Valley several times a week using VOIP. Also, I know of a retired British couple, now living in the Caribbean, who now use Skype to keep in touch with friends and family.

Sell your shares in all the big telecom companies, VOIP is bad for their health!

Yes, it's a whole new world out there. If all of the above sounds a bit daunting, don't be discouraged. Believe me, it's really much easier than it seems at first, once you get your learning curve up and going. Don't forget: *l'appétit vient en manageant!*

KEEPING IN TOUCH VIA E-MAIL

You might just say, "I don't know anyone with e-mail". You would be surprised how many non-business people, housewives, students, maybe even your own children can now be contacted by e-mail because of the growing popularity of PCs, the unreliability of the postal services (how many letters just never arrive?) and the pleasure and benefits of instant delivery of communications. E-mails arrive in your correspondent's ISP server within seconds, waiting to be downloaded by their PC.

To organize e-mail, contact an ISP who will issue you with a personal address of your own choice, say, your own name plus the ISP reference linked with the email sign, @ (it's on your PC keyboard), such as gregorypeck@ aol.com. With this permanent address, you can send, and receive, e-mails around the globe at local call telephone rates or free if you have a fixed monthly fee arrangement with your ISP.

Beyond all doubt, one great feature of e-mail nowadays for a retired person is the flourishing circulation of humorous mails around friends, former colleagues and family. Rare is the week when I fail to receive a batch of e-mails from friends, often originating from far-off places and containing splendid humour both by way of text and some with great photos and drawings in colour. What a lovely way to stay in contact with others, through an e-mail which raises a chuckle when they least expect it and brightens up their day, followed by a happy retort to you. And the great thing about e-mails is that you can send copies to multiple correspondents, simultaneously, and edit incoming mails and re-transmit copies to friends and relatives.

If e-mail permits you to stay in touch with old friends, it also enables easy communication with experts on matters of mutual interest. In my own case, after researching the art of calligraphy for chapter 11, The Art of being a Cultured Person, I e-mailed a draft of my text to a teacher of calligraphy and author of a book on the subject, whose name and e-mail address I found on the internet. This expert reviewed what I had written and came back to me by return e-mail with some excellent advice as input to the text. Yet another example of the ease of communication arising from the new digital age.

You can even receive and reply to e-mail when

travelling by linking your portable PC to the telephone socket in your hotel room, or, as previously mentioned, your mobile phone, which will automatically dial into your personal mailbox at your ISP and download any mails pending.

As previously mentioned, you can also transmit digital photos by e-mail (See chapter 8, Going digital).

As a final word on the ease and efficiency of sending messages via e-mail, a new communication tool for travellers has sprung up along with the internet. I am referring to the now familiar sight of cyber cafés in towns and cities all over the world.

Travelling without your portable PC but want to send an e-mail or look up something on the web? The answer is, pop into a cyber café and use one of their computers for a modest fee.

I have a young family member who took a sabbatical after studies and backpacked around South America for several months. Through his using cyber cafés along his route through Brazil, over the Andes and down to Paraguay, he was able to send regular e-mails updating me on his adventures.

Suggested reading:

Beginner's E-mail Book
   by Helen Smith.

WRITING, STORING AND PRINTING TEXT AND IMAGES

Writing text

Here are some comments on using the Word programme if you want to try writing a novel or short story, or merely write letters or notes.

If your spelling ability occasionally falters, after all nobody's perfect, the Microsoft Word software has a built-in spell check which automatically signals spelling errors for correction to give you a fault-free text. Want to check on the word count of your new novel? That is also available in the Word programme.

A computer dispenses with the hassle of changes traditionally associated with pen and paper, such as use of an eraser or tearing up a page and starting all over again and thus saves time and patience. One wonders how prolific writers like Victor Hugo and Walter Scott, working with quill pens dipped in ink every few words, no room for errors, coped without computers. Just goes to show what really gifted and spontaneous writers they were.

Inserting pictures into text

Here is another example of the versatility of a PC once you are more experienced. One option is that you now can insert pictures into written text.

If you are writing, using your PC, about, say, a visit to the Louvre in Paris, you can log on to www.louvre. fr, go to "selected works", transfer a picture of the Mona Lisa to your text, placing it exactly where you want, and either print the completed text in colour or send it off by email. A word of warning about using pictures and text extracted from websites if it is your intention to use such data for a published work. Many websites are protected by copyright laws. In today's litigious market place, crawling with copyright lawyers eager to make money for their clients, it is best to seek a website author's permission before going public with any extracts from the internet.

Printing hard copy

To run off a hard copy of your PC-stored text, you need to link a printer to your PC. There is a wide range of mini-sized printers on the market that transfer PC-stored text and photos to normal A4-sized paper in black and white or colour. For colour printers, the normal ink-jet version is cheap to buy but, like Mr Gillette who sold razors for peanuts and made his money selling blades, cartridges for ink-jet printers can be expensive for frequent copies.

Another option for regular printing is the laser printer which is more expensive to purchase but more economical to run.

You should note that PCs have to be specially programmed to operate with any given brand of printer. Make sure that the computer shop where you buy the printer will carry out the necessary programming to your PC.

BUYING AND LEARNING TO OPERATE A PC

When buying your first PC, it is sometimes tempting to respond to ads for mail order supply direct from the manufacturers, at first sight at a better price than your retail computer store. This approach can have its drawbacks. A mail order PC may arrive at your home with the main operating programmes still on CDs requiring to be assembled before you can get started to use the machine. You may end up at your computer store, apologising for not having purchased the machine from the store but begging the chap to put the machine in working order and give you some lessons about how to use it.

So, by far the best approach by a newcomer to computing is to buy your PC at your local computer store with a series of introductory lessons from an expert as part of a package deal. If you opt for the self learning route to operating a PC, there is a vast choice of books available. Here are a few chosen at random:

Personal Computers for Beginners: a Low Tech Guide to High Technology
   by Joanne Woodcock
Learning to Use Your Computer
   by Angela Bessant
Computer Basics (The Complete Idiot's Guide)
   by Joe Kraynak

If you are a retired and happily living couple, here is a word of advice about going it alone in home computing. Be prepared for your loved one to question your being "constantly" so engrossed in the screen and keyboard and "oblivious" to well meant small talk that doesn't quite register, such is the pleasant concentration that operating a PC brings to the user! So why not both of you get your own PC and share the pastime and the pleasure of learning more from the internet?

When starting, take my advice and adhere to the "KISS" principle (Keep It Simple, Stupid!), and learn the basics at first: basics being: using the keyboard to create normal word files, sending emails via Outlook Express and logging on to the web with Internet Explorer, or perhaps merely your special interest such as digital photography. If you choose to learn through tuition, get a spiral notebook and take lots of notes of the various moves by keyboard and mouse to achieve each application so that later you can refer to these notes when working the PC on your own. Then progress through experience and self-learning. It's an engrossing and rewarding pastime. And, to be frank, being able to operate a PC works wonders for one's self esteem.

Above all, pay no heed to the many older people around us who are sceptical of the excellence of the internet, merely because of their own unwillingness to get to grips with personal computing and try it out for themselves. The internet is today's answer to knowing more, instantly. Like only recently, a summer visitor here in Spain asked me about the current state of the potentially prolonged legal battle in the European Court of Human Rights in Strasbourg of British, German, French and Spanish owners of property further south in Valencia who have had parts of their land seized by real estate promoters and are being forced to pay out large sums for road, lighting and sewage developments, under a new "land grab" law issued by the provincial government. He added that he had heard that one retired English couple is said to be threatened with a compulsory bill of over £80,000 for a road which is planned to run through land adjacent to their house! Knowing absolutely zero about the case and mightily intrigued, I proceeded to surf the web and eventually tried the website of The Times newspaper, where I keyed in "Valencia" in the search box and found a lengthy report stating that....well, why not find out for yourself where these unfortunate homeowners stand, once you are in the driving seat of your new PC?

CHAPTER 6

Protecting the Planet

BY JOINING THE ACTION TO IMPROVE THE ENVIRONMENT

This chapter outlines ways for being positively occupied to ensure action is being taken to create a more healthy and sustainable environment for future generations.

REACTING TO REPORTS ABOUT THE ENVIRONMENT

Much is said in newspapers, on television and the internet about the environment. One has to approach this information with caution. Facts come in many shades of grey and there are lots of statistics for this hot topic. Is the source of the information credible and how were the numbers arrived at? Are the facts and statistics being presented in a fashion which is biased to influence public opinion, one way or another? Are, perhaps, certain items of "news" not just the result of journalists hyping a story; scientists seeking more funding or, indeed, the limelight; politicians vote catching; overstatements by conservation organizations to arouse public opinion; or simply long haired, bearded "greens" stirring things up? Bear this in mind when weighing up your opinion as to whether or not what is said is a major issue.

"THAT THE NEXT CENTURY MAY EXIST"

The French-Canadian astrophysicist Hubert Reeves is a senior research adviser with the National Centre for Scientific Research in Paris and is also a respected environmental campaigner and author.

In a collection of Letters to Future Generations by scientists and philosophers published on the UNESCO website, Mr Reeves warns that "this twenty-first century will be green, or there will be no twenty-second century".

Mr. Reeves explains that "...these words refer to the threat posed to life on earth by human activity in all its forms. One only needs to mention the words deforestation, desertification, air and water pollution, the greenhouse effect, and the destruction of the ozone layer on the one hand, and the exhaustion of natural resources such as petroleum, gas and coal on the other, to become conscious of the disasters that are piling up at an ever faster rate".

He goes on to say, "In parallel with this, we are witnessing a rapid and dynamic increase in environmental awareness. This movement is attempting to slow down and stop this planetary destruction by taking specific measures and by organizing international conferences devoted to research into technologies for environmental protection and sustainable development. The stakes could not be higher. The survival of the human race, as well as that of innumerable animal and plant species, are in the balance. In this regard, the twenty-first century will be crucial".

Mr. Reeves concludes by an appeal, "Let us make certain that there are still people around to celebrate the start of the twenty-second century. The responsibility for this lies with all of us."

HOW YOU CAN BE INVOLVED?

As you read this chapter, you might want to consider how your existing contacts with organizations, companies and people could help generate the kind of action which Mr. Reeves and many other environmentalists are talking about. And also consider if you might want to take an active part with the many groups of private citizens who are already putting pressure on governments and business leaders to generate change.

FOR A BETTER PLANET, WHO DOES WHAT?

Government action

Most governments of developed countries are concerned about the state of the environment and are trying to achieve a delicate balance of implementing new measures for better conservation and, at the same time, trying to avoid excessive hardship for those people who earn a living in the sector concerned. An example: placing quotas on fishing catches that directly affect the livelihoods of fishermen and their families.

Government leaders are often faced with strong opposition from business groups such as the big oil, electricity, chemical and food corporations who may see conservation programmes as an impediment to their core interests: making profits for shareholders and maintaining employment. After all, corporations provide employment and contribute the lion's share of cash to finance the economy. Also, when it comes to the crunch, government leaders may bow to the demands of companies that participate in the funding of political parties, and this is what counts when political decisions are in balance. This is particularly relevant in the US which, as we shall see later, is the world's top polluter.

It is encouraging to note that, recently, a group of leading companies, which include the oil giants, BP and Shell, have made an appeal to the UK government to formulate, as a matter of urgency, a long term policy to combat climate change. The root cause of this appeal is that, recognizing that action must be taken to curb climate change, these big corporations have to know as soon as possible planned government moves in order to adapt their long term business plans accordingly.

Given the restraints on government action on effective measures to improve the environment, who in our society is keeping environmental damage high on the agenda to ensure that there are no lapses in the momentum for change?

Non-government organizations (NGOs)

In the 1960s, those memorable years of the anti-Vietnam war protests in the US, student riots in Paris, and the new sounds of the Beatles in Britain, a growing awareness that the excesses of modern life are destroying the environment gave birth to a number of independent conservation groups, known as non-government organizations or NGOs, with a charter to instigate popular calls for governmental action to implement remedial action.

The NGOs cited in this chapter are a few examples of where you might participate to support courses of action which can improve the planet for generations to come. There are many, many other NGOs not mentioned that warrant research to identify which one would correspond most to your ideals and lifestyle.

Now let's look at some of the major environmental issues on which remedial action is required and how everyone can become involved.

THE POLLUTED AIR THAT WE BREATHE

We should first and foremost consider the harmful effects of the ever increasing emissions of toxic gases on our health, especially in the cases of the sick and elderly.

The biggest contributors to air pollution in the EU are emissions from the exhausts of cars and trucks, coal and oil-fuelled electricity generating stations and iron ore smelters and civil aviation. New member countries in eastern Europe are major polluters because of their antiquated fossil fuel burning plants. Not that we are much better here in western Europe, having our fair share of smoke stacks belching black smoke, countless trucks emitting diesel fumes and traffic jams in our congested cities.

Emissions from road transport consist principally of oxides of nitrogen (NOx) and carbon monoxide which is later oxidized in the air and converted into carbon dioxide (CO_2), generally referred to as "carbon emissions". These pollutants have harmful health effects, mainly respiratory, and are particular hard on asthma sufferers. Burning fossils fuels for power generation and smelting ore also produces sulphur dioxide (SO_2) which can have adverse health effects such as nervous disorders, heart and kidney damage.

In the world's industrial heartlands, clouds of NOx, from car and truck emissions, and SO_2, from burning fossil fuels in industrial plants and power generators, are carried, sometimes across continents, in the wind, dissolve in rain and become what we now know as acid rain. Acid rain erodes buildings, kills forests and plants and pollutes rivers and lakes, reducing fish stocks, and causes lung ailments and breathing difficulties.

Developed country governments have now put in place measures to reduce NOx through laws to fit catalytic converters to new vehicle exhausts, and reduce SO_2 by placing special filters on the smoke stacks of fossil fuel burning installations, all in an effort to reduce pollutants. Whilst this seems to be succeeding in reducing the frequency and toxic content of acid rain, there is still a long way to go in persuading all nations, especially in the rapidly growing economies of Asia, to comply with these measures to improve the air that we breathe, given the global effects of toxic gases which know no frontiers.

The manufacture of cement, after water the most globally used material, is a prime producer of carbon dioxide emissions. It is estimated that the kilns making cement, which involves heating raw materials such as limestone and clay at 1000°C, emit a tonne of carbon dioxide for every tonne of cement produced. And cement manufacture is reckoned to be responsible for some 5 to 10% of global carbon emissions. When you consider the frenetic pace of construction of new buildings in countries like Spain, Europe's number one user of cement, you have to conclude that the EU has concrete reasons to invest more funds to back initiatives in research into more environment-friendly alternatives for traditional cement. Could one of our grandchildren be the inventor of a cement substitute and the future Bill Gates of the 21st century?

Civil aviation, rapidly growing in volume because of the popularity of low cost flights, is a major source of pollution, with emissions of CO_2 and NOx. A recent report by the UK's Royal Commission on Environment Pollution stressed that air traffic is a significant producer of greenhouse gases. One odd aspect of air transport which particularly irks environmentalists is that aircraft fuel escapes the normal government taxes levied on oil products.

Environmentalists argue that tax-free aviation fuel is a prime factor which allows airlines to provide low cost flights, many tickets at the equivalent of the price of a meal in a decent restaurant, thus increasing the demand for air travel in Europe and the consequent polluting emissions. By taxing aviation fuel, governments could reduce the burgeoning air traffic and raise finance to combat the overall build-up of greenhouse gases from all sources, that is, industry, power generation, households, road transport and aviation. It has been estimated that, in Britain alone, taxing aircraft fuel at the same rate as petrol for cars could raise a mighty £9 billion for the Treasury coffers to spend on necessities such as public health care.

REDUCE AIR POLLUTION AND LIVE LONGER!

The WHO (World Health Organization), based in Geneva, recently issued a report, announcing statistics that left me in admiration of the sheer creativity of those who compiled them, no doubt using mainframe computers, masses of data networked from other remote computers, advanced mathematics and simulation software.

The WHO report informed us that air pollution reduces the life of the average European by, wait for it, 8.6 months, due to accelerated deaths from cardiovascular and respiratory ailments. The current EU plan to reduce pollution by 2010 (I assume, notwithstanding the pollution from new members from the ex-Soviet bloc) should give us all an extra 2.3 months before the Reaper's arrival on our doorstep. The last mind-boggling number is that the EU pollution reduction plan will economize €161 billion in health costs. Wow! The only factual item in the entire statement is that diesel-fuelled trucks, trailing toxic fumes and crawling like ants around Europe, are the main polluters.

GREENHOUSE EFFECT AND
GLOBAL WARMING

To understand global warming we have to be clear about what is meant by the expression "greenhouse effect".

The greenhouse effect is a natural relationship between the earth and the sun, which for centuries has given us acceptable temperatures and climate. Solar energy impacts the earth's surface and, in turn, the earth radiates heat back into space creating, in the process, a temperate climate.

Like a greenhouse whose glass panels trap solar heat once received, certain gases in the atmosphere, notably carbon dioxide and methane, trap some of the outgoing energy rising from the earth's surface. Methane, by the way, is a highly inflammable natural gas. Quantities of methane are released into the atmosphere from oil extraction, coal mines and landfills, and other natural means such as volcanoes, swamps and what is termed "intestinal gas" from livestock such as sheep, cows and buffalos. Indeed, it is said that bovine bowel emissions are released around the world in such high volume that this is one of the main reasons why we are in such deep....well, I won't use the word, you know what I mean, about the alarming upward trend in the levels of greenhouse gases! Methane is about 50 times more potent than carbon in the greenhouse effect but, whilst carbon has a life of many centuries, methane fortunately disappears within only a few years.

In early 2006, German scientists at the Max Planck Institute in Heidelberg made the environmental news headlines by announcing that they had discovered that plants and trees in tropical climates, normally considered as significant absorbers of carbon dioxide, may emit large amounts of methane. Their scientific paper ventured that this hitherto unknown phenomenon may account for between 10% and 30% of the total global methane emissions. This has come as a shock to climate scientists who are now examining the basis for the German claim and speculating how, if true, this aberration could have been excluded from the science of biochemistry for so long. Similar but uncorroborated claims that have been made in the past about rising levels of methane in the Amazon rainforests tend to lend credence to this startling new theory.

Latest scientific findings indicate that the levels of CO_2 and methane in the atmosphere are currently at their highest levels during the last 650,000 years. These are the conclusions of a new EU study by climate scientists examining gases trapped in the ice cap three kilometres below the surface of Antarctica. CO_2 is reckoned to be up 30%, with methane 130% higher than at any point over that vast expanse of time. This has resulted in an overdose of the greenhouse effect, and, as discussed later, an increase in global warming.

OPTIONS TO REDUCE GREENHOUSE EFFECT

Road transport

To reduce the emissions of carbon and other gases from the world's ever increasing population of cars, buses and trucks, researchers are working on the development of cost-efficient biofuels which include diesel fuel made from various oilseeds, now referred to as biodiesel, and technology to reduce the use of petrol, to be replaced by ethanol which is extracted from sugar-cane, corn, maize, wheat and soya beans.

None of this is new science. When Rudolf Diesel exhibited his engine at the World Exhibition in Paris in 1900, it ran on peanut oil! In Brazil, a major producer of sugar, 80% of new cars sold today can run on ethanol as well as petrol. In Britain, biofuel is catching on with, for example, a new fleet of 40 Ford Focus police cars in Somerset powered by ethanol, distilled from locally grown grain. Ethanol from grain is claimed to produce 65% less greenhouses gases but provides performance comparable to a petrol-driven engine.

Another alternative to using petrol and diesel fuel to power buses, trucks and cars, and also incidentally home heating and light, is hydrogen, in the form of fuel cells, battery stored power units. Hydrogen is a climate-friendly source of vehicle power which was discovered in the 19th century but discarded when the auto industry focused on the internal combustion engine. One of the prime sources to generate hydrogen is water, using electrolysis. If, however, burning fossil fuels such as coal or oil are used in the electrolysis process, hydrogen loses its carbon-free advantage. Clean and sustainable sources of energy such as solar and wind can also be used in hydrogen production but not in sufficient volume needed for today's vast vehicle population. Another source of hydrogen is methane, that abundant and potent greenhouse gas, which can be split and hydrogen extracted but leaves CO_2 which has to be disposed through underground storage methods still to be developed.

The hydrogen-powered road vehicle with its efficient acceleration and silent combustion may well have an environment-friendly future in the long term if clean solutions can be found for volume production of hydrogen itself. At least it will reduce our excessive dependence on the potentates of oil-producing countries.

One immediate solution to reduce emissions of greenhouse gases from cars and trucks is the return to favour of using diesel engines for road transport. The revival of diesel is due to the recent development of a new low-sulphur fuel which is cleaning up considerably exhaust emissions and which heralds a brighter future for the diesel engine on tomorrow's roads.

Another way forward to reduce road transport carbon emissions and our addiction to oil is without doubt the "plug-in" petrol-electric hybrid engine for cars and trucks. The way the plug-in hybrid works is that, when in town, the vehicle is powered by an electric battery, charged from the mains electricity overnight, and, on the open road, the driver switches to petrol for greater speed. Clearly, early adoption of the hybrid vehicle solution by as many road users as possible is a must because inner-city transport, with its traffic jams, is a major culprit for high carbon emissions.

The most telling impact of hybrids will be the blissful reduction of noise levels of the infernal combustion engine which insidiously pervades our daily lives in heavily populated areas. Am I wistfully dreaming when I already hear the deep crackling noise of protest from bulky bikers, revving engines as they sit astride their Harley-Davidsons, when new laws are announced forbidding the use of petrol combustion for motor bikes in inner cities and foresee the glee of the long suffering silent majority who note that noise abatement is finally taking place?

Since current battery technology gives a vehicle only 30–50 miles before recharging, the main challenges that vehicle manufacturers face are to develop batteries in sufficiently dense form to extend mileage and produce the vehicles at prices competitive to traditional petrol technology.

We also have to find cleaner ways to generate the electricity needed for our new plug-in hybrids.

ELECTRICITY GENERATION

Nuclear power

Providing for the world's growing needs for electricity will mean building more nuclear fission reactors, with the hazards that this presents. Nuclear technology, when used for peaceful purposes such as power generation is one of a number of environment-friendly alternatives to fossil fuels since nuclear plants do not emit carbon and other polluting gases.

Another plus for western nuclear technology is that nuclear power plants are relatively safe and major accidents are rare. France is a case in point with its roughly 75% reliance on nuclear power for its electricity needs and a high score for accident-free performance. On the other hand, the UK has a relatively low, many say too low, 20% nuclear contribution to its overall energy needs.

The widely reported core reactor meltdown, the most dangerous type of nuclear accident, at Three Mile Island in the US in 1979 was a notable exception in the west. Chernobyl in the Ukraine, the greatest nuclear disaster ever, in 1986, was an indication of the threat that the ex-Soviet bloc nuclear legacy poses to our society.

Even if we consider that, in the west, our nuclear plants are safe, radioactive leaks, that can occur from storage of waste, are dangerous to human health. High exposure to radioactivity is, in one word, fatal. And nuclear waste has a radioactive life of thousands of years.

To sum up, the compelling argument against nuclear fission reactors is that of disposing of nuclear waste. In countries like France and Britain, spent nuclear fuel from around the world is being reprocessed to extract usable uranium and plutonium, leaving behind highly dangerous radioactive waste. Currently this waste is stored above ground, which represents a potential danger to present and future generations.

Burying highly radioactive waste deep underground, at a depth of at least 500 metres, is probably the only logical solution. But what municipality is going to approve of such a lethal pile of doom in its vicinity? Therein lies the dilemma for local and government leaders. In 2006, Finland was one of the first countries to embark on this underground "final" solution for its nuclear waste, at a site which has had fault-free nuclear reactors for the last three decades, giving the burial project better acceptance by the local community.

Suggested reading on this hot topic:

Britain's Nuclear Waste
by S Openshaw
Accidents Will Happen: The Case against Nuclear Power
by the Environmental Action Group

A new generation nuclear solution
After years of tortuous debate, a global consortium of governments, the US, EU, Japan, China, Russia and South Korea, finally signed, in 2005, an agreement to proceed with the development of the International Thermonuclear Experimental Reactor (ITER). The ITER research project will be based mainly in France, employing the best scientific brains from around the world, and, if successful, will pave the way for the construction of nuclear fusion reactors for commercial electricity generation.

Nuclear fusion differs from fission technology inasmuch that it does not produce long life lethal radioactive waste. In fact, nuclear fusion waste is harmless. The fusion process, which is the same power as that used by the sun and other stars, the laser and the H-bomb, involves as principal fuel a heavy isotope of hydrogen which is derived from plain water. If that sounds simple, the challenges of achieving nuclear fusion will be enormous since the process requires massive volumes of hydrogen to be heated to a temperature in excess of that at the core of the sun, that is, in excess of 15 million°C (see chapter 9, Stargazing). All of which is estimated to take up to 30 years of research with a budget of $12billion: cheap at the price if it ever works.

Natural gas
During the 1990s, countries in the EU, in a "dash for gas", switched to natural gas as a means to reduce the dependence on coal and oil for power generation, although it also generates significant, albeit slightly lower, carbon emissions. In the UK, natural gas accounts for about 40% of the total fuel used for power generation. That other natural and greenhouse gas, methane is also being captured from coal mines, landfills and waste plants for power generation.

An abrupt realization during 2005 that the EU is largely dependant on Russia, our erstwhile cold war foe, as its main supplier of natural gas and who can turn off the tap at a whim, is causing most countries to rethink the natural gas option.

Clean coal technology
Given the world's huge reserves of coal, the main alternative to a nuclear solution for emission-free energy generation is what is termed clean coal technology or CCT. Currently, CCT is very much in its infancy and is the term used to describe a process whereby coal will be converted to a gas, as opposed to burning the coal in a power generator, burned to power a turbine and carbon emissions captured and stored geologically either underground in disused coal seams or under the sea, in

depleted oil and gas reservoirs or saline aquifers which are located below the earth's surface.

Most major industrialized countries are now investing large sums in R&D of carbon capture and storage which should, if all goes to plan, go on stream in volume within ten years to reduce emissions of greenhouse gases.

Another solution, now being implemented, for reducing carbon emissions is improving the efficiency of boilers in coal-fired power stations by using less coal to generate the required heat energy. State-of-the-art boilers also now permit the burning of "biomass", the term used for all plant matter such as trees, grass and agricultural crops, to be used as a solid fuel or in gaseous form as a clean mix with coal.

Renewable energy
The alternatives to fossil fuel, gas and nuclear are what is termed renewable energy such as wind, solar and hydroelectric from dams and rivers, tides and waves. Some have drawbacks. Solar energy in northern Europe has its obvious limitations and wind farms, spoiling the contours of the countryside and noisy, are acceptable only as long as they are not in one's own backyard. On the other hand, tidal energy plants, sunk in the sea or river estuaries but still in their infancy, have enormous potential because, once built, they are cheap to operate, need no fuel, and tidal movements are as regular as clockwork, ten hours a day, all the year round.

CONSEQUENCES OF INCREASED GLOBAL WARMING

Since the increase in greenhouse gases has resulted in an overdose of the atmospheric heat trapping process, this has caused a steady rise in temperatures around the globe which is likely to accelerate global warming.

Meteorologists are studying the possibility that the increased frequency of very strong hurricanes is due to global warming. Hurricanes, called typhoons in Asia, and cyclones, which are violent hurricanes of limited diameter, develop when tropical seawater, with a surface temperature of in excess of 26°C, evaporates and massive amounts of moisture rise and mix with up to 150mph winds and air pressures, causing a violent spinning in the eye of the storm. Sea-surface temperatures are rising, probably due to global warming.

Higher temperatures are raising ocean levels, fed by rivers of melting glaciers on mountains such as the Andes and the Himalayas, and the polar regions of Antarctica, Arctic and Greenland. The ice sheets of Greenland, which cover an area of 1.7 million square kilometres, an area roughly the size of Mexico and rising to a height of three kilometres, are melting and dumping hundreds of cubic kilometres of fresh water into the North Atlantic annually. The sea ice in the Arctic is at its lowest point for more than a century. Melting of the ice sheets of the western coastline of the Antarctic is also a cause of steadily rising ocean levels.

It is estimated that some 20 billion tonnes of water are added to the world's oceans each year because of melting ice sheets. A "drop in the ocean", you might say, but with sinister implications over the long term for low-lying heavily populated coastal areas around the globe.

In the Himalayas, where there are over 3,000 glaciers representing one of the world's largest latent reservoirs of fresh water, scientists have noted a substantial glacial retreat over the past decades with an increase in the levels of glacial lakes, the main source for the River Ganges.

Some scientists are predicting that one effect of global warming may be, paradoxically, a colder climate in northern Europe within perhaps decades, due to a perceived weakening in the flow of the Gulf Stream. The warm ocean current of the Gulf Stream flows north-easterly from the Gulf of Mexico, giving off massive atmospheric heat to northern Europe. On its arrival at the Arctic Ocean, the Gulf Stream cools rapidly and is augmented by freshwater from melting glaciers and rainfall feeding rivers flowing into the sea. Scientific measurements indicate that the returning southward current is slowing down considerably, possibly due to this increased freshwater content. Some scientists fear that, if this trend persists, it could result in the demise of the Gulf Stream over time with a permanent lowering of all year round temperatures in Europe.

In general, global warming is likely to create extreme weather conditions, with heavier rain, but at less frequent intervals, in winter and hotter and more arid summers, with longer periods without any rain at all in many parts of the world.

MOUNTING WATER CRISIS

What are the other potential consequences of global warming? Many experts are concerned that higher temperatures could eventually have a critical impact on water supplies in many parts of the world. For example, already there are much publicized signs of severe water shortages in China with its vast population of more than one billion and rapidly growing industrialization.

The World Bank recently released data on internal freshwater resources of global industrialized nations, as measured in cubic metres per capita of population. The country having the highest water reserves is Norway, followed by New Zealand and Argentina. The countries having the most critically depleted reserves are China, Spain and Japan.

Water storage in most countries is unevenly distributed because heavy rainfall geography does not always correspond to high population areas. In Britain, for example, the biggest demand for water is in the southeast part of the country whereas the heaviest rainfall is in the lesser populated northwest. More pipelines are required around the world to transfer water resources to where they are most needed.

If the world's glaciers continue to melt because of rising temperatures, most of the water runoff will end up in the sea unless there are sufficient dams and reservoirs to collect water from swollen rivers before reaching coastlines, and store these supplies for needs during increasingly arid summers.

It is difficult to see how non state-owned water companies can be motivated to make the substantial capital investments in new dams, reservoirs and pipelines for the long term future needs of society and incur the high costs to replace existing leaky and obsolete pipelines if they cannot be guaranteed a satisfactory return on investment through higher prices to consumers. The potential for future critical water shortages and the need for massive capital investment represent a strong case for increased state aid for financing of water infrastructure, with distribution operations managed by leading publicly quoted water companies, who have the expertise to reduce leakage, upgrade reservoirs and pipelines, trim operating costs and manage efficiently collections from customers to provide profitable financial returns for re-investment and to shareholders.

Many government and municipal water monopolies do a poor job of planning for the future and delivering water and sewage services simply because of the absence of pressures of competition.

As a shining example of how large publicly quoted water companies can reshape the world's badly run water facilities, a few years ago, Suez Lyonnaise, one of France's leading water companies, took over a water concession in Buenos Aires by acquiring an inept Brazilian state utility in financial difficulties. Suez invested $1billion of its own capital to upgrade the infrastructure and expanded distribution of water to 1.6 million consumers, in this case, without raising water prices but by reducing operating costs. In La Paz, Bolivia, Suez Lyonnaise took on another water concession and, by installing improved management and bringing in and training poor local people to the labour force, reduced operating costs by two-thirds and improved water distribution to customers.

A CONTROVERSIAL WATER RELOCATION PROJECT IN SPAIN

As an illustration of how planning for redistribution of a country's water resources can meet with vehement public opposition, a recent Spanish state hydrological project provides an interesting case study for future attempts in the EU to tackle water shortages, brought on by global warming, by channelling water to drier, more needy parts of a country. A recent Spanish government report warned that large tracts of southern Spain may turn into desert because of climate change, inefficient irrigation by farmers and the increased water consumed by booming tourism.

The project was to divert 100 billion litres of water annually from the River Ebro to other, more arid parts of Spain. The Ebro has its source in the northwest mountains inland from the Atlantic coastline, with its heavy rainfall, and runs east through Zaragoza in the province of Aragon and flows into the Mediterranean at Tortosa, (about 150 kilometres south of Barcelona). From points near to the Mediterranean coast, the water was to be diverted northwards to Barcelona and southwards to the arid belt in the regions of Valencia, Murcia and down as far as Almeria in eastern Andalusia, all vibrant tourist areas with thirsty hotels, leisure complexes, golf courses and many homes with swimming pools. The watering of a golf course alone, and there are lots of them all along the coast, consumes between one and two million litres a day. Spain's population of golf courses has doubled to 276 over the last five years, with a further 150 planned, to attract the top spending tourist trade.

Equally important, the eastern hinterland of Spain has thriving farmlands, supplying fruit and vegetables to markets in northern Europe, with huge needs of water for irrigation which swallow up two-thirds of available resources. And because water in Spain is really cheap, only a tiny fraction of consumer prices paid in other parts of the EU, wastage is abundant.

The infrastructure of the plan called for the building of 120 dams and 1,000 kilometres of canals and pipelines at a cost of 18 billion euros, one third funded by the EU.

The plan unleashed a storm of protests. The Ebro Delta is an extensive lagoon-spotted nature park and sanctuary for breeding and winter stopover of migrant birds, including flamingos and herons. The very existence of this unique wetlands habitat was threatened by the plan and environmentalists protested in their thousands with massive demos, in Tortosa itself and Madrid, Barcelona and Zaragoza and even a rally outside the EU headquarters in Brussels.

Further inland along the River Ebro, people protested that they would be forced from their homes by building of dams and flooding of valleys. Three villages, two centuries-old churches and part of the ancient pilgrim's route to Santiago de Compostela were going to disappear under water!

Conservationists rightly protested that it was not so much more reservoirs that were needed but improved efficiency of ways to avoid losses of water such as more efficient methods of irrigation, mainly by using drip irrigation as opposed to flooding, and less wanton wastage by consumers.

In 2004, the voices of protest prevailed and a new, incoming government voted to scrap the project entirely and replace it with an alternative programme, with a vastly reduced capital investment, to build fifteen desalination plants along the eastern seaboard, leaving the Ebro Delta untouched. Not that this is an ideal solution either, since as pointed out below, this will result in increased carbon emissions from fossil fuel-hungry desalination plants.

WATER, WATER EVERYWHERE, NOR ANY DROP TO DRINK

These immortal words by Samuel Taylor Coleridge, 19th century English poet, are no longer valid. Desalination plants are one of the keys to providing a solution to the water shortages forecast for the future, by using seawater to produce fresh drinking water.

Desalination does not come cheap and has its downside. The plants involve substantial capital investment and are energy-intensive, with the carbon gas emissions that burning fossil fuel entails, and leave mountains of brine for disposal.

Alternatives to using fossil fuel for desalination include nuclear power, available only in developed countries, and renewable energy solutions such as solar, wind and waves. Poorer nations, probably those who will be most in need of water, will require massive financial aid from rich countries to install and operate desalination plants.

It is evident that severe water shortages could have dire consequences in terms of human, animal and plant lives. The plain fact is, no water, no life. To add to the potential gravity of the situation, some think-tanks are suggesting that a world water crisis could lead to so-called water wars, similar to a seizure of territory to secure a source of oil. Just think of the number of rivers around the world where upstream neighbouring countries are hostile and you have a potential clash over water rights.

Making it rain

Another way to alleviate severe drought is what one might term precipitating precipitation by what the meteorological scientists call "cloud seeding". How often have you stared wistfully at cloudy skies hoping for some rain to water your parched garden, especially if there is a hosepipe ban in force?

There are literally oceans of fresh water vapour in the atmosphere, but only a small fraction reaches the earth as rain or snow. Invented back in the 1940s, cloud seeding is a method to tap these immense latent, celestial reservoirs of water. The way this is done is to inject particles of silver iodide (or salt or dry ice) into clouds either by projecting them from the ground or by dropping from aircraft. Water droplets attach to the particles forming snowflakes which then melt into rain as they reach lower altitudes. The trick is to get the right kind of clouds and ideal conditions to provide just the acceptable quantity of rainfall and not torrential rain which can cause chaotic flooding and damage.

China and Thailand, both countries experiencing the severest drought in the last fifty years, are currently carrying out extensive cloud seeding projects to provide drinking water and badly needed water resources for their crops and booming industrialization.

Pressing for action on future water crisis

The Swiss-based global NGO, World Wildlife Fund (WWF), well known for its splendid panda logo, is only one of many conservationist groups pressing for urgent action to counter the threat of global warming to the world's water resources. In a plea to a UN Conference on Climate Change, held in Milan in 2003, where delegates from 180 nations attended, WWF warned that the world's glaciers could melt within a century, if global warming accelerates, leaving millions of people desperately short of water once these latent sources of water supply are depleted. WWF is working with scientists who are monitoring the melting of glaciers in the Himalayas and was also very active in gathering public support to oppose the Spanish government plans for diverting the waters of the River Ebro.

WWF, which boasts five million supporters worldwide, depends on public support, including volunteers, for its campaigns which include the water crisis, climate change and wildlife conservation. To know more about getting involved, contact can be made either at WWF-UK, Panda House in Godalming in Surrey or via its website, www. wwf.org.uk.

Members of the public can also play a major role by backing the politicians and business leaders who shape future policy for water. Here are some of the main aspects of policy which have to be at the top of the global agenda for water.

Most experts reckon that at least $100 billion a year has to be invested globally over the next 25 years to avert a water crisis of major proportions. Much of this may have to come from the private sector which therefore needs public support. Our politicians have to be persuaded to treat investment in water as a priority not an option.

Well-meaning government water subsidies currently worth billions of dollars to industry and, above all, farming, only encourage squandering of water. This is especially the case in the US. These subsidies should be replaced by realistic price increases to all consumers. Once people recognize the true cost of water, they may start to take conservation seriously, turning off taps and sprinklers, treating water with respect.

Governments must also provide incentives to oblige farmers to employ sub-surface drip-feed irrigation instead of flooding fields to water crops, one of the prime culprits of water wastage in volume.

In short, water, that formerly abundant basic element of our daily lives that we have always taken for granted, has now emerged as a prime issue for action by all to assure the future survival of life on our planet.

KYOTO PROTOCOL

The Kyoto Protocol, which became effective beginning 2005, commits the 141 industrialized nations who have signed up to the treaty to reduce their emissions of greenhouse gases by 5% and over (EU is set at 8%) below 1990 levels by 2012. The treaty only became effective after Russia had agreed to join. Russia's entry was vital for the treaty to be activated, because it had to include nations accounting for 55% of global green-house gas emissions and Russia is reckoned to run up 17% of the total global pollution output. A major deficiency in the original Kyoto agreement is that it does not include agreements binding countries to reduce aviation emissions, that important and growing source of greenhouse gases.

Those polluters not joining the Kyoto club

The United States, which produces about one quarter of global pollution, is not a signatory to the Kyoto Protocol, stating that any immediate attempt to cut carbon emissions would be harmful to its economy and create millions of job losses.

In 2005, the US and Australia, two of the main opponents to the Kyoto Treaty announced the formation of the Asia-Pacific Partnership on Clean Development and Climate whose adherents also include China (the world's second biggest polluter and soon to be number one), India, Japan and South Korea. In total, these nations, all highly dependent on coal for energy needs, account for almost one half of the global population and one half of greenhouse gas emissions.

The aims of the Asia-Pacific Partnership are mainly focused on the development of clean coal technology and the transfer of CCT, which will take up to a decade to develop fully, to emerging industrialized nations.

The agreement is voluntary on the part of all signatories and entirely technology-based and sets no targets to curb greenhouse gases today or in the future. Why should these nations invest mega-dollars in clean technologies if there are no economic incentives? Over the intervening period, carbon emissions will continue to be on the increase in the Asia-Pacific region, especially in China and India.

We can only wait to see how the trend of global warming develops over the next decade and if the global political resolve to reduce greenhouse gases produces tangible results. Recent indications are not promising. By the end of 2005, most countries in the EU not only failed to cut emissions of CO_2 but these were on the increase. Only the UK and Sweden were ahead of target. All countries, particularly Ireland, Italy and Spain, now have to increase investments in renewable energy projects and clean technologies if they are to meet their Kyoto pledges by 2012.

To learn more about climate change, here is some suggested reading:

The Long Summer: How Climate Changed Civilization
by Brian Fagan
Global Warming: the Complete Briefing
by John Houghton
The Heat is on: Climate Crisis, the Cover-up, the Prescription
by Ross Gelbspan.

WHERE ARE WE HEADING TO COMBAT CLIMATE CHANGE?

Given that most of the thinking world has now accepted that carbon emissions must be curbed to halt the momentum of climate change, how are our governments reacting as regards medium to long term planning for carbon emission-free sources of power generation?

It is clear that renewable energy sources such as solar, wind, waves and tides can only provide a minor, but valuable, contribution to the energy needs of the future, because of the ever increasing power required to fuel industrialization and to serve the consumer needs of a rising global population.

The upshot of the above debate is that most governments of major industrial nations, in the US, Europe and China, have opted for the nuclear fission power route to combat climate change. Already, the total number of nuclear power plants around the world stands at 440 (of which roughly one quarter are in the US) and this total should increase over the next decade. That rising industrial power giant, China already has nine nuclear plants with a planned expansion of a further thirty to supplement its ever increasing burning of coal.

The nuclear power option would make sense were it not for the major danger to human security that it presents with its inexorable build-up of lethal nuclear waste, for which no secure disposal solutions have been implemented. Currently most, if not all, waste is stored above ground presenting the evident dangers of radiation to human and animal life.

It is precisely in this area where public pressure has to concentrate. We must persuade governments to invest more resources to find ways to activate extensive geological storage, that is, disposal deep underground, for nuclear waste in the interests of the security of present and future generations. This disposal should involve not only the burgeoning waste from nuclear power generation but also from the hordes of obsolete nuclear weaponry littering the world at large.

Within the EU, there is a mixed bag of forward planning of measures to be implemented to combat global warming by limiting the emissions of greenhouse gases and reducing our reliance on oil and fossil fuel for energy generation.

To cite notable examples, Finland has embarked on the construction of a major nuclear fission plant, with an underground repository to store the nuclear waste. France also continues its high reliance on nuclear power for future energy requirements. And Germany is engaged in a rapid expansion of renewables, with huge investments in the construction of wind farms and installation of solar panels. Belgium is studying the possibility of storing its nuclear waste underground in a project ingeniously-named High Activity Disposal Experiment Site (HADES).

At the time of writing, Britain is involved in an extensive public debate as to whether the country will build new nuclear fission plants, each of which takes ten to fifteen years to build and then has a working life of about another fifty years. This debate is spurred by credible predictions that, by 2015, power generation from nuclear, natural gas, fossil fuel and renewables will fail to meet national needs by possibly as much as 20%. As an island state, the country has abundant natural potential renewables from wind, waves and tides which must be harnessed to meet future power needs.

Scotland is one area of Britain having high ambitions to implement the potential from wind, wave and tidal power generation. The stated aim from the Scottish Executive is that 10% of electricity generated in Scotland by 2010 will come from the sea, the equivalent to replacing a major fossil fuel power plant. Their long term targets are that wind, waves and tides should provide up to 40% of total electricity needs in Scotland by 2020.

Currently the British government has allocated funds to finance research and development of technologies for carbon capture and storage to reduce emissions from coal-fired power stations and industrial plants.

One easy way to stay informed, with updates on this ever-evolving scenario of the fight against climate change is to log on regularly to the BBC website www.bbcnews. com (see chapter 5, Surfing the web), and click on to Science/Nature where you will find the latest news by their environment correspondents.

Here is a final thought. Are the world's governments and the public at large taking the threat of global warming seriously? Could it not be, as suggested by a new book just out, The Weather Makers, by Tim Flannery, that, since homo sapiens' origins are from tropical climates, now migrated to colder climes, the word "warming" has positive overtones in the public mind in the colder, northern hemisphere of the developed world? Therefore, had an even colder environment been the issue at stake, concerted action to counter the threat of climate change would have been given top priority long ago.

GETTING INVOLVED IN ENVIRONMENTAL ISSUES

Amongst the many conservation groups campaigning for action to prevent climate change and the related issue of the way forward for power generation, one of the best known is Friends of the Earth, which describes itself as an international environmental pressure group. With its headquarters in Amsterdam, FoE has its main UK base in London.

FoE is active in monitoring UK government policy on nuclear power and, in particular, the operations of British Nuclear Fuels plc (BNFL) and its programme for reprocessing dangerous and unwanted spent fuel, coming in from other countries, particularly since the UK has currently no long term disposal facilities for high level nuclear waste.

In the area of climate change, FoE is active in urging restraint in air travel expansion in order to limit environmental damage. It rightly states that UK air travel is soaring, and, if unchecked, is probably set to more than triple in volume over the next 30 years. To compensate for this rapidly growing aviation pollution, the UK industry and power generation sectors, households and road users will have to produce vast cuts in their carbon emissions, if the country is to meet its Kyoto Protocol targets. FoE's Right Price for Travel campaign is working to persuade the government to instigate a tax on aviation fuel to dampen growth in demand for air travel. FoE is also campaigning to sway public opinion to persuade the government to reduce drastically its plans for airport runway expansion such as Stansted and Heathrow.

In another aspect of climate change, FoE works for the promotion of alternative sustainable sources of electric power, and more consciousness of the need to reduce energy consumption in homes and/or using renewable energy sources such as solar and wind power for homes. In this latter respect, FoE is promoting public awareness of Energy4All, a community owned wind farm project, currently in four areas of Britain. FoE is also promoting public awareness of government grants to install solar panels in private homes to generate household needs, with possible sales of surplus electricity to power companies.

FoE welcomes all sort of participation by its members in the many projects to improve the environment, including volunteering to research for more intelligence to be used for its campaigns in lobbying governments and business for controls over dangerous chemicals, cleaning up rivers and many other issues on the agenda for protecting the planet. Only recently, an FoE spokesman was quoted by the BBC as welcoming the decision by Buckingham Palace to invest in "green" power by building a £1million hydroelectric power station at Romney Weir on the River Thames for the electricity needs of Windsor Castle.

FoE has community discussion forums for local groups of members throughout Britain and in 71 other countries around the world. FoE is an interesting way to meet new people, with mutual interests, wherever you live.

Friends of the Earth's website, www.foe.co.uk quotes The Guardian newspaper as referring to it as "the UK's most effective environment group". Praise indeed.

VOLUNTEERING TO PROTECT THE PLANET

Another way to join the action is by linking up with one NGO which seeks volunteers to work in the field to collect information to assist scientists and conservation groups to combat changes that are taking place in our environment, including climate change.

The NGO is Earthwatch Institute. Founded in 1971 in Boston, Earthwatch Institute is a scientific-based global environmental NGO with overseas offices in Australia, Japan and the UK. Earthwatch Institute (Europe) is registered as a UK charity with its office in Oxford, which opened in 1990. Earthwatch's global mission is defined as a commitment "to conserving the diversity and integrity of life on earth to meet the needs of current and future generations". In other words, to address all changes on the planet which may adversely affect life now and in the future.

The core activities of Earthwatch are environmental research and education, raising awareness and generating action, achieved through part-time volunteers working in tandem with their scientists on varied projects, which can involve travel to interesting spots around the globe. Field research projects include climate change, greenhouse gas reduction, threatened species, identification of new species in tropical rain forests and conflict between human and wildlife needs.

Earthwatch research reports are shared with partnerships such as multinational corporations, governments, the academic community, United Nations, UNESCO and conservation NGOs. Volunteers also assist with content for newsletters to members of Earthwatch to raise awareness, and fund raising. Funding of Earthwatch activities is provided by multinational corporations, foundations, government donors and by public donations.

In addition to volunteering, Earthwatch (Europe) also organizes expeditions for paying members of the public interested to join discovery projects and learn more about wildlife. Examples: projects involving sea mammals such as whales and dolphins, seals, basking sharks, and otters. To find out more about volunteering and discovery expeditions, you can log on to www.earthwatch.org or contact their office in Oxford. As mentioned in chapter 3, Digging up the Past, Earthwatch also has expeditions to archaeological sites.

TIMM...BER!

What forests do for our environment

It has long been accepted that the world's forests contribute to the reduction of greenhouses gases by absorbing carbon dioxide to satisfy the natural need of trees for carbon (trees are roughly 50% carbon) and releasing oxygen as a bi-product of their growth. Now, climate scientists are having to rethink this golden rule on two counts. First, an exception to the carbon-in, oxygen-out rule was that, during the 2003 heat wave in Europe when temperatures soared 6°C above normal, trees and plants exuded much more carbon dioxide than they absorbed, thus adding to the build-up of greenhouse gases. The second reason for a rethink of forests as climate-friendly is the possibility that, as mentioned earlier, the tropical rainforests may be in fact a significant generator of methane, that potent greenhouse gas. If further studies prove this to be the case and not merely the preliminary findings by a small team of climate scientists, the methane factor could alter many of the ground rules of the global fight against climate change.

When vast tracts of forests are levelled, and the trees burned, to make way for croplands and pastures and to provide domestic fuel, the carbon stored in the trunks is released into the atmosphere as carbon dioxide. Burning wood as a result of deforestation, especially in vast quantities in the tropical rainforests in Africa, SE Asia and South America, particularly the Amazon rainforests in Brazil and Bolivia, is considered by researchers to be a significant contributor to the total of global output of greenhouse gases.

Suggested reading:

Trees and Woodland in the British Landscape
    by Oliver Rackham
In the Rainforest/Report from a Strange, Beautiful, Imperilled World
    by Catherine Caufield

Getting involved in tree conservation

If you are a tree lover and wish to ensure that our forests and wooded parklands are given every priority for their conservation, why not consider joining The Woodland Trust, Britain's leading woodland conservation charity? Already with around a quarter of a million adherents, the charity has a charter to protect ancient woodlands, increase new woodland developments and promote public enjoyment of trees. TWT has now over 1,100 woodland sites in its care, covering 45,000 acres of land and offers activities for the public ranging from walks around its woodlands, tree planting and public consulting on woodland conservation.

Volunteering

Volunteering is welcomed for all sort of activities, such as fund raising, organizing awareness events and guide walk leaders for rambling in TWT woodlands. For more information on this splendid pastime involving the love of trees, consult www.woodland-trust.org.uk.

To end this brief account of the rapidly deteriorating state of our planet, let me remind you of some of the words of a song, sung by the American folk singer, Tom Paxton, entitled *Whose Garden was This?* and which can be heard on his CD, released in 2005, Tom Paxton Live in the UK.

Whose garden was this?
It must have been lovely,
Did it have flowers?
I've seen pictures of flowers,
And I'd loved to have smelt one.

Whose river was this?
You say it ran freely
Blue was its colour
I've seen blue in some pictures
And I'd love to have been there

Oh, tell me again I need to know
The forest had trees
The meadows were green
The oceans were blue
And birds really flew
Can you swear that was true?

CHAPTER 7

Pardon, Monsieur le Matelot

LEARNING A SECOND EUROPEAN LANGUAGE

Funny thing about languages, one would have thought that the logical course for humanity would be for us all to speak the same tongue, but this is not the way life panned out. Since the beginning of man, people have huddled together in tiny groups and invented their own way of communicating, quite at odds with others chattering away on the other side of the mountain.

Linguistic historians reckon that during the centuries BC, when there were only around ten million people in the world, there were perhaps over 10,000 languages spoken. No one knows why people of one country want to do their own thing when it comes to speaking. At present, with a world population of six billion, there are estimated to be just under 7,000 languages spoken worldwide, of which the extinction rate is something like two a month. The vast majority of the total languages are spoken by small groups, mostly in Africa and the Pacific region. Only a dozen or so languages are major players around the globe.

The undisputed leader, way ahead of the pack and wearing the yellow jersey, so to speak, is Mandarin Chinese with around one billion speakers. Put another way, of the total world population, one person out of six speaks Chinese. Makes you think. Given China's fast becoming a global economic powerhouse, this would seem to be an excellent choice of second language for our teenagers, the businessmen of tomorrow. Even if English may be the language of international corporations, the way to succeed in business is to speak the tongue of the market place.

More or less equal in second place with 300–400 million speakers is English (with the US), Spanish (with South America and the growing Hispanic population in the US) and Hindi (India has a population of more than one billion).

The table of the top eleven world languages published by UNESCO shows French and German sitting in the last two places, with under 200 million speakers; although French is shown to have a high proportion of users as a second language, given France and Belgium's colonial past in Africa.

A SECOND EUROPEAN LANGUAGE

Setting aside the world linguistic scene, the rest of this chapter is directed to those English-speaking readers who cannot yet speak a second European language and who want to integrate with life in mainland Europe, with its unique cultures varying from one country to another.

First, we shall look at why learning and practising a second language would make sense as a retirement pastime and then examine some of the more practical aspects of adopting this addition to your social skills, which will open new opportunities to meet people of differing lifestyles.

As a starter, here is an amusing tale about an Englishman, let's call him George, who made up his mind to learn French and enrolled for a course at the Berlitz School of Languages in London. His game plan was that, once he had completed the course, he would take a holiday in France to test his new linguistic skills.

After several months of intensive tuition, George

boarded the Eurostar bound for Paris. On arrival at the port of Calais, he got off the train and looked around him. How to test his French? Ah, a bar, go in and get myself a beer. "Bonjour, Monsieur, une bière, s'il vous plaît." Good day, Sir, a beer, please. Gee, great, got that one right, as the barman duly pours his beer. Feeling very pleased with himself, George retired from the bar, glass in hand to sit down at a table.

At the next table, a group of French sailors were drinking beer and chatting noisily. George eyed them enviously. If only he could find an opportunity to join in the conversation. Then it happened. A fly, which had been buzzing around their table, suddenly came down and plopped into one of the sailors' beer. George perked up. What an opportunity! "Pardon, Monsieur le matelot, il y a *un* mouche dans votre bière." Excuse me, Mr sailor-man, there's a fly in your beer. The sailor turned to George and said, with a friendly grin, "*Une* mouche! Delighted that his French neighbour had responded to his contact, George cried out, "Quelle vue remarkable!" What remarkable eyesight!

Which all goes to illustrate the pitfalls of the masculine and feminine nouns in certain tongues and that how one letter only, a solitary "e", can cause a communication fog between people of different languages in Europe.

WHY A SECOND LANGUAGE?

Medical researchers are becoming more and more convinced that the mind benefits from the mental exercise of practicing a second language. A report which appeared recently in The Economist and which made this point was accompanied by photos of two bi-lingual statesmen in their seventies, Jacques Chirac of France and Kofi Annan of the UN, both still able to maintain punishing daily schedules despite having clocked up a lot of mileage in life. The message from medical research is therefore that a second language will do wonders to keep your mind alert and active.

Fine, I hear the argument from English-born speakers that most educated mainland Europeans and people in the tourist industry all speak reasonable English so why bother? Besides, inevitably the EU will adopt English in time as its common language. Here are some counter arguments to these well founded statements.

Languages are all about culture and are the result of many, many centuries of developing distinct and unique styles of enjoying life in each individual European country. That is why the EU may never accept a common language such as English because it would mean diluting priceless and vital cultures.

Many say that the future of Europe is being multi-lingual like the Swiss, many of whose nationals speak three tongues, Swiss-German, French and Italian. Ah, would we all have their talent for languages!

That said, the argument for one language only for the EU to promote better integration is pretty compelling. All major European multinational companies, such as the giant Siemens of Germany, Nestlé of Switzerland and Alcatel of France, have plumped for English as their internal corporate language, used for interdivision memos, telecoms, emails, in-house meetings and so on. A case of a corporate strategy for better internal communications in a multi-lingual group to maximize efficiency which takes priority over cultural differences.

Which, I hurriedly add, does not get you off the hook. If retired or near so, you should be keener on cultural contacts than corporate efficiency!

Another prime reason for picking up a second language

is the ability to open new horizons to meet people of different nationalities. Oh, I hear you respond, but many of them speak English!

Around Europe, the majority of even well educated people are more at ease when speaking their own language, especially at a purely social gathering. Often they do not want to make the effort during a whole evening of finding the right words in your language in order to communicate with you. Even more so if you are the only foreigner present. Certainly, if the subject of conversation turns to sensitive subjects such as politics, many people, especially southern Europeans, will involuntarily switch to their own language to express their feelings volubly.

So, if you want to meet people from other countries, do them the courtesy of learning at least a basic comprehension of their mother tongue. This will be much appreciated, especially coming from an Anglo-Saxon, a race noted for their insularity about other languages. Moreover, unless you prove your wish to communicate in a second language, you may not be invited to join groups of people of that language on social occasions.

Typically, around Europe at international meetings, where the *lingua franca* may be English, during leisure time people tend to slip into groups of their own country or culture, such as the French-speaking (French, Swiss and Belgian) or the German-speaking (Germans, Austrians, Hungarians and other Eastern European countries). This is to avoid the hassle of conversation where long explanations may be necessary to communicate clearly. This is also true of the likes of golf and tennis clubs where gatherings in the bar after a game naturally split up along national and language lines.

So, the golden rule around Europe is that as long as you are seen to understand most of what is being said and can respond with simple phrases, you are much more socially acceptable. Trying to force your own language on people may last a few minutes but then die a natural death as the language of the majority reinstates itself.

THE (LACK OF) EUROPEAN UNION

One has to feel some healthy scepticism about the quality of cohesion of the Brussels Commission and the European parliament when delegates from twenty-five countries are squabbling in fifteen official languages, backed by an army of interpreters, all to grab a bigger slice of the EU multi-billion euro pie.

Think about the scenario. Delegates coming from opposite ends of the continent, from Helsinki, way up near the north pole, to Rome, at the heart of an excitable and voluble country, and from Lisbon, on the Atlantic coast, to Budapest astride the Danube, all communicating in their very own way of words and sounds, expounding that, no way we can cooperate, our voters would never accept, but give us more euros all the same! When one word, one tiny word, wrongly interpreted, can trigger off a whole host of misunderstandings, creating hurt feelings, resentment, injured pride, you name it. Isn't it time for us all to learn at least a second language?

The people who live on frontiers, called *frontaliers* in French, have an advantage, being brought up with two or even three languages. That said, languages can provide vent to political convictions. Take the Flemish, for example. Since they are Belgian, a bi-lingual country, the Flemish are educated in both French and Dutch but you don't hear much French spoken in Antwerp.

A colleague of mine, a Parisian, was in Antwerp on business, and was walking back to his hotel but got lost. Spotting a Suit with briefcase, he asked, in French, for directions. The Flemish person replied "Do you speak English?" and proceeded to give him directions in broken English. And evidently this was not an isolated case. When I mentioned this at a dinner party, a Belgian lady present told us that when she worked for a multinational pharmaceutical company, based in Brussels, she telephoned and talked, in French, to a university professor in Antwerp to discuss a technical matter, he replied in similar terms, "Can we speak English, please?" Like the Catalans and the Basques who do not want to speak in Castilian Spanish and so on.

Yes, so much for the European Union. Boy, what a misnomer when it comes to languages.

ABOUT SWITCHING LANGUAGES

Which brings me to an important point if you are going to learn to speak a second language. Let me give you an example of when not to switch languages although there may be a valid reason for doing so. Our friend George, now reasonably competent in French, has a business meeting with a French customer visiting England. The French person begins the meeting in rather poor English. Should George switch to French? Courtesy dictates no, to avoid the insult of inferring that the Frenchman, and a customer no less, "don't speak no good English".

George's best tactic is to reply first in slow, clearly enunciated English, avoiding any colloquialisms. Then, and only then, he should ask permission to switch to French, saying, I am a student of your beautiful language. George will have made a friend for life, if I know the French.

WHAT EUROPEAN LANGUAGE TO CHOOSE?

If your choice is open, better opt for a second language

which you learned back in your schooldays. That way, you may be able to recollect some of the grammar, especially the conjugation of verbs, useful things verbs, and much more complicated in other Euro-languages than in English.

Then again, more likely, your choice may be dictated by your vacation choices or that property on the Mediterranean coast you bought for your retirement in the sun.

Building up your vocabulary

The most effective approach to building up the vocabulary of your chosen language is researching all the key words that are essential to your particular lifestyle. Let's take an example. You have bought for your retirement an old farm cottage in, say, rural Tuscany, or somewhere inland along the Côte d'Azur or up in the mountains behind the sun-soaked coast of the Costa Brava and want to renovate and furnish it to your taste and style.

With the aid of a dictionary, research the kind of vocabulary you will need to go to the nearest village to choose, say, those pink linen curtains just right for the bedroom or try to find special tiles from a local builder's yard to decorate the old kitchen, and all the hundred and one items that would bring modern lifestyle to an old domain. Research some of the basic vocabulary for electrical items like light bulbs and wall lamps, the kind of paints and brushes you will need to restore to cheer to the doors, ceilings and walls, with your choice of colours, and all those garden items you will need like an electric lawn mower and, of course, plants galore, grass seed, whatever to bring the garden to life. Then you need to learn the whole gamut of numbers to understand and discuss price quotes adequately. With a simple grammar book, learn the basic verbs such as to have, be, come, go etc with their conjugations for past, present and future to tag these along with the nouns to build up simple sentences such as "do you have...or, when can you come to our house... or, how much does it cost?"

Jot all this down in the spiral notebook you have bought specially for the purpose and look at it from time to time and commit to memory. Go through the list of vocabulary as many times as your memory needs to put all away in permanent storage for later retrieval.

May I offer a suggestion? Why not view the film Under the Tuscan Sun where Diane Lane plays the part of an American who leaves the States and buys an old house in Tuscany to start a new life? Although the film is mainly in English, there is lots of Italian spoken: *che bella lingua*! It might tempt you to start to learn Italian and, who knows, buy a place under the Tuscan sun for your retirement.

Pronunciation

As you periodically peruse your spiral notebook for your new vocabulary, read out the words aloud, seeing each object in your mind's eye – logs for the fire, daffodils, a pair of rubber boots – and try to get your tongue around the words so that they come out as foreign sounds, not foreign words pronounced in English. Try to get a patient friend who speaks the language fluently to help with the pronunciation. Film actors imitate accents, why don't you try to drop your English public school drawl or your Glaswegian vowels and try to talk like an Italian, Frenchman or Spaniard? Give it a go, it can be a lot of fun. Start by trying to imitate Maurice Chevalier saying, "Tank 'eaven for leedle gerls," with his strong French accent.

Now you are ready to go out into the market place with a measure of confidence in your ability to communicate in your new second language, avoiding supermarkets where no conversation is needed but using small markets and shops as a language lesson combined with shopping. Have with you that essential pocket dictionary and your spiral notebook in your pocket or handbag as a hidden understudy to bolster your confidence!

There is a splendid anecdote about General de Gaulle and his wife, who were persuaded by their aides to learn to speak some English out of courtesy to the Allies and were attending a banquet at the British Embassy in Paris. During a lull in conversation, he turned to his wife, Yvonne and said, for all to hear, "My dear, what is ze greatest thing in life?" His wife replied "A penis, of course." An embarrassed silence ensued, until the General said, "My darling, you forget, the English pronounce the "h", you say hap-pi-ness!" All a question of pronunciation.

Reading foreign-language press

As a means of building up your vocabulary in your chosen second language, you should consider starting to read a newspaper in that language, such as a magazine which summarizes the highlights of a week's news with also articles on sport, books, theatre, cinema, fashion, and other aspects of the country's cultural life. Examples of magazines to read: *Le Figaro* Magazine from France, *El País* weekend supplement from Spain and *Der Spiegel* from Germany.

This is a way, not only to learn new ways of saying things in your second language, but also to learn about what is happening in the country of your second language; news and developments which most probably are not reported in your own national press or television.

Armed as always with your dictionary, read the articles which interest you most, look up words which you don't understand and, if potentially useful for your interests, jot them down in your notebook. Run an eye over the notebook from time to time to ensure that all these new words get truly embedded in your memory for instant delivery when next required.

Bi-lingual books...and CDs and DVDs

A couple of Parisian publishing houses that I know of, there may be more, have come up with a very pleasurable way of permitting their readers to extend their vocabulary by reading works by classic authors with English on one page and a French translation on the opposite page. You can therefore read as much as you can understand of the French text and, where you hit a phrase that needs translating, all you have to do is refer to the page opposite. If you judge that any words or phrases could serve your lifestyle, make a note for future reference. As examples, two books which were given to me by a French lady, who runs a chain of bookshops in Paris, were:

Collection of short stories
   by Graham Greene:
Editions Robert Laffont
The Crack-Up and other short stories
   by Scott Fitzgerald:
Gallimard

At last, there is now a way to learn a second language which combines the pleasure of reading top authors.

There are also now available to students of languages CDs in which a story is narrated in two tongues, the advantage over books being that the listener also learns pronunciation; and DVDs where you can select to view a film in the (dubbed or original version) language which you are learning with sub-titles in English to assist understanding, or vice-versa.

If, during your language learning process, you want to immerse yourself in a multicultural and multilingual atmosphere for a couple of pleasant, often hilarious, hours in sunny Barcelona, try to see *L'Auberge Espagnole*, (UK title Pot Luck) a French film released in 2003 and involving a group of seven university students from seven different EU nations, all attending studies in Barcelona under the Erasmus programme and sharing a large and untidy apartment in the city centre.

L'Auberge Espagnole, a French expression meaning "you only get what you bring in", and literally The Spanish Hostel, features at the start a young French student, Xavier, who leaves Paris for Barcelona under the Erasmus Student Network programme, an organization devoted to developing student exchange between EU countries and directed to internationally minded students to learn other languages and cultures. Once in Barcelona, during his search for a flat, Xavier meets up and moves in with the other students, English, German, Italian, Spanish, Belgian and Danish, who are already sharing the apartment.

See the film in its original version, with subtitles in your own language, and follow their bright and amusing conversations, mainly in French, Spanish and English, as they gradually bridge the cultural gaps of each of their native countries and merge into a cohesive group of friends. Listen to the accents of your chosen second language and try to copy mentally and vocally.

After seeing the film, you might ponder: could not the likes of the Erasmus programme be an ideal education for your grandchildren to grow up as multilingual Europeans with a better understanding and respect for other European cultures?

Who was this Erasmus, you might ask? Desiderius Erasmus, born in Rotterdam in 1466, was a truly multicultural European. After his education at a religious college near Gouda, he spent some time as the private secretary to the Bishop of Cambrai and, after taking priest's orders, went to Paris to study and take up teaching. Amongst his pupils was an English aristocrat, Lord Mountjoy, who invited him to Oxford where he stayed for two years. By 1500 Erasmus was back in Paris and then, six years later, he was in Padua in northern Italy, acting as tutor to Alexander, Archbishop of St. Andrews, son of James IV of Scotland. Then Lord Mountjoy again persuaded Erasmus to go and live in England, teaching in Cambridge as professor of Divinity and Greek! From 1514 onwards, he lived in Basel, then back to England and then on to Louvain in Belgium. He is chiefly known academically for his many religious works amongst which were his annotated New Testament and his edition on St. Jerome in nine volumes. A remarkable pan-European scholar and humanist and most worthy to have an EU student exchange scheme named in his honour.

THE "YOU" IN EURO – LANGUAGES

When learning a second language, you have to grasp what lies behind innocent words like *tu/vous, tu/vosotros, du/sie* et al, with regard to the degrees of familiarity around Europe when addressing an individual.

To illustrate the subject that I am embarking on, let's use a French example. In France, when talking to someone you have just met and you want to say, "how are you?" you do not normally use the familiar "tu" but "vous". Fine, you probably know that already. But, did you know that the Spaniards are much more relaxed about the "tu" taboo and use it much more freely amongst peers? Nonetheless, as a beginner, you are better to stick to the *vous/usted* formal approach until you get to know the person and leave it up to he or she to suggest the switch to the more friendly "tu" use. This is an area of human relations which is totally alien to the British, having the multi-function and dispassionate "you" at their disposal for communications. On the other hand, that other person's nod to the use of "tu" is a sign of pleasure in your company and to be appreciated.

Be careful also about the use of first names in countries like Germany and France whose polite society has certain taboos about the kind of liberalism in respect to the immediate first names nowadays in Britain and America when first meeting someone. The "Hi Jurgen/ François" greetings when meeting someone for the first time in Germany or France could raise eyebrows in polite society.

Interesting to note that, when I worked with a German company, in meetings, English was spoken because I and other non-Germans were present. My German colleagues used first names freely, including their own. During a break, however, when the Germans had switched to their own language, very often they reverted to *Herr* when addressing one of their colleagues. Strange place, Europe!

LANGUAGE LEARNING CURVE

You should normally find that your learning curve for a second European language runs roughly as follows.

The initial phase is that you will learn to speak more than you can understand is said to you. This is normal, right? As you progress, you should enter a new phase when you will start to understand much more than you have mentally archived to speak in your second tongue. Hopefully, with lots and lots of practise in meeting people and talking their language, there should be a narrowing gap between understanding and speaking.

TRYING OUT YOUR NEW SKILLS

Let us imagine a simple scenario, like George in the opening paragraph entering the bar in Calais: you step on stage for the first time to try out your new language. The first rule is don't panic or get flustered if the first time you speak in your new language the other person says, "don't understand", shaking their head. The chances are that they had their mind on something else when you addressed them or, hopefully not, you were looking down instead of face to face with the person, mumbling in an unsure sort of way!

Let us also assume that you are in the Basque country of Spain and would like to buy a pair of shoes and enter a small shoe shop in Santander, after having made all the preparations of nouns and verbs to be used. Calmly put your mind into Spanish mode and think through your proposed conversation like an actor going on stage.

Preface your delivery with a pleasant, "Buenos dias," which should get the shop assistant's full attention. Look the assistant straight in the face and say slowly, enunciating clearly what you have rehearsed, no apologetic grimaces to infer, look you may not understand what I'm trying to say but bear with me! If necessary using the odd hand signal to help get the message across in the initial confidence building phase of speaking your new tongue.

Watch the accent, try to imitate the sounds of the people round about you.

"Buenos dias, tiene usted un par de zapatos, en mi tamano, quarenta y uno, con cordones, marron y bastante leger para este tiempo de primavera" etc. Good morning, do you have a pair of shoes, in my size, forty one, with laces, brown and fairly light for this spring weather etc.

Our friend George succeeded in mastering a second language, despite his initial skirmish with the French fleet in Calais, why not you?

CHAPTER 8

Going Digital

PROCESSING DIGITAL PHOTOS BY COMPUTER

If you are contemplating digital photography as a pastime, combined with printing your own photos, or taking a step further and processing the photos via a PC, doing your own editing, and then printing or screen display or perhaps transmitting through the internet, read on.

If you are not yet skilled in the use of a PC, the possibilities offered by digital photography for an absorbing retirement pastime might well justify your buying a computer and taking some lessons from a local PC dealer. A retired friend of mine did just that and became highly skilled in processing his digital photos by PC. With the confidence and know-how gained from digital photography, he soon easily graduated to other applications such as email and internet on his new home computer.

Nevertheless, if, like some retired people, you are firmly against the thought of getting into computing, you can still process and print your digital photos at home by acquiring a special printer for colour photos. This is explained later in a bit more detail.

This chapter will give you an outline of the basics of digital photography; choice of cameras, that is, performance versus what you are prepared to spend; how you might go about editing photos for special effects; doing your own printing on paper; presentation on PC screen; and online transmission by e-mail to friends and family.

WHY GO DIGITAL?

For those of you who, like me, are enthusiasts of traditional photography and are perhaps sceptical about going digital, here are two possible reasons to give digital photography a closer look. With digital you can:

- see each shot immediately after it is taken and decide if it is the picture that embodies the interest of the subject you seek. If not, you can shoot again until you have what you aimed for. With traditional cameras, you can perhaps shoot a whole roll of film and you will not know the results until you have had the film developed and printed and even then you may not have what you wanted.
- edit your pictures using sophisticated computer technology to arrange and present the picture to emphasize the most interesting elements, eliminate the undesired and even merge items from other pictures.

Now let's look at traditional versus digital in more detail for the benefit of newcomers to photography.

PHOTOGRAPHY BEFORE DIGITAL

The art of photography has come a long way since the camera set up on a tripod and operated by a chap bent forward, legs astride, with head under a black cloth peering into the lens, photographing the high school class of '53, in black and white, later tinted in sepia, those splendid brown tones used in the early to mid-1900s for special effect.

The golden years of the sixties and onwards saw the introduction of the Single Lens Reflex or SLR camera with 35mm film, used by amateurs and professionals alike to take great pictures using lenses ranging from wide angle for landscape shots, to short and medium lenses with zooms for close-ups taken from a discreet distance.

Here now is a brief reminder about the technical aspects of a camera lens, a necessary element for discussing the various options to taking good pictures with a digital camera.

A camera lens operates with two variables: the degree to which it can be opened or closed, called its aperture, and the speed of exposure of the film to the quality of light, called the shutter speed.

The degree to which the aperture is opened determines the depth of field. A shallow depth of field aperture setting will produce a photo where the principal subject is in clear focus with the background less clear or hazy. This is the type of shot where, say, you want to shoot a photo of a person amongst a crowd and not have the crowd in focus. A greater depth of field aperture setting will give a picture of clear focus of all elements of the scene.

The shutter speed will determine how clearly you wish to catch an action scene with, or without, blurred edges of the principal (moving) subject. Take the case of photographing a golf shot at the moment when the club head strikes the ball. Here an ultra fast shutter speed, expressed in fractions of a second, is required to capture a clear image of impact, diluting to the extent possible, the blur of speed.

Also, light conditions, bright sunlight or dim light,

determine the best shutter speed, with poor light requiring a slower speed so that the film can absorb the image shapes and tones adequately to make a quality picture.

Our forefathers, pioneers of photography, had to learn to adjust the lens aperture and shutter speed to take great pictures.

If all of this is causing you some concern because it is a bit technical, relax. Nowadays, most cameras, including digital cameras, are equipped with auto-focus lens, which, thanks to technology incorporating battery power, will size up light conditions, distance of subject from the lens and self-adjust to take a clear picture with full depth of field. Note, however, that manual adjustment is still necessary to take shots where the subject is moving at high speed or you seek variable depth of field.

The drawback of the old SLR camera, for all its superb qualities, is that in-house development of film and printing requires a well equipped darkroom, which, for the amateur enthusiast, means setting aside a special room. And for transmission over the internet, SLR photos have to be "digitalized" via specialized equipment called a scanner.

There was also "instant" photography with the introduction of the Polaroid, with its point-and-shoot action and, seconds later, a (relatively poor quality) print emerging from the camera.

DIGITAL PHOTOGRAPHY

New generation digital photography is a quantum leap from traditional photo technology with films requiring skilled darkroom development or Polaroid-type instant prints.

Popular low-cost digital cameras are equipped with an auto-focus lens and an inbuilt image recorder or "sensor", dispensing with the need for camera film and providing life-long multiple picture exposures. And there is, on most models, a "flash" for taking indoor pictures, probably the most popular use of this kind of camera, such as taking shots of guests at an evening dinner party.

Unlike SLRs, with digital cameras you do not normally have to get your subject in focus by putting one eye to the camera and looking "through the lens", (after having hoisted your specs above your forehead!), but now you can hold the camera away from your face and see the shot you intend to take through a window. Good news for those who wear specs.

This window in the camera also provides you with an instant view of each shot after it has been taken, with a choice of "reject and erase", or store for processing and printing. The cameras come with the connecting cable and software necessary to transfer the pictures stored in camera to a personal computer.

These are the "pluses" of digital cameras. One of the "minuses" is that digital cameras operate entirely on battery power. So, they are like mobile phones, if the batteries are run down, they just don't work. Fortunately, to decrease the expense of continually buying new batteries, many models are equipped with rechargeable batteries and a charger like mobile phones. Another major "minus", as we shall see later, is the limited capability of low price digital cameras in taking fast action pictures.

BUYING A CAMERA

How do you choose the "right" camera, quite apart from price considerations? The first thing to learn is the importance of "pixels". Pixel (short for "picture elements") is the term used to describe the mass of tiny dots, which go into forming a digital picture. Pixel power, denominated in millions or "megas", dictates the quality and ultimate size and resolution of the final pictures.

For example, a camera with one million (or "mega") pixels will only produce high resolution effect photos of roughly postcard size on your PC screen or paper. Larger prints from this pixel rating tend to be less sharp. A digital camera of three to four megas and more, are naturally more expensive, and will produce sharper large-sized, say A4 size, pictures. The more pixels, the better the clarity and sharpness of your pictures. As they say: if you pay peanuts, you get monkeys! That said, as the volume of the market for digital cameras rapidly increases, prices are becoming lower and lower.

As seen above, even low-cost digital cameras have an in-built auto-focus so there is no need to twist the lens to get your subject into focus like in the old days of the first SLRs, but they do have one drawback as regards taking fast action pictures. Before each shot, to activate the auto-focus, you have to depress a button on the camera, usually the shutter button. In low to medium price digital cameras there are distinct pauses between your pressing the focus button, and then depressing the shutter release and getting the image "sensor" response. Thus, taking shots of acceptable quality of, say, your grandson taking a drop kick, at the instant the foot makes contact with the ball, turf spurting, are very difficult to achieve.

The manufacturers of new digital photo technology offer optional solutions to the above drawbacks by producing two different ranges of cameras.

Point-and-shoot cameras

The first, which are the most popular low-cost models,

with auto-focus lens and therefore what are called "point-and-shoot", are digital cameras with resolutions of one to two megas for normal-sized snapshots and others up to three to four megas and therefore capable of high resolution pictures of up to A4-size. These models are great for landscapes, pictures of friends whooping it up at parties and the like.

But, if you are going for actions shots like a tussle-for-the-ball scene at a football match, taken from the spectator stand, neither of these models is for you.

Professional cameras

The second, more up-market and expensive models are four to six megas, or more, digital cameras (which look a bit like traditional SLRs) for better resolution pictures with "see-through-the-lens" focusing, zoom lens and which are, optionally, auto-focus or manually adjustable. Now, you are in the right ballpark for creative depth of field and action pictures. But, again, there is a caveat. The camera high pixel count creates problems at the level of computer storage and online transmission, which can only be solved by "compression", which means diluting the number of pixels of each picture.

More about this later.

PROCESSING PHOTOS VIA A PRINTER

If you only wish to print out your photos on paper, you can achieve this without using a computer. You will find that there is a broad range of digital photo printers on the market for amateur enthusiasts which not only enable you to download your pictures from your camera and produce excellent colour prints but also serve as normal copiers and scanners (which convert old photos taken with a traditional camera to digital form).

A word of caution at this point. Before launching into printing your own photos you should study the costs involved as opposed to having your photos printed by your local camera shop.

The paper required to produce glossy or matt prints of photos, which comes in various types, can be relatively expensive. And once you buy a certain make of printer you may be tied to that manufacturer, and their prices, for the ink cartridges, which can involve significant expense, particularly colour cartridges. So, look before you leap!

USING A PC TO PROCESS DIGITAL PHOTOS

As we shall see later, a PC enables you to edit photos to highlight the better features of each shot and eliminate what you don't like, create a photo library in the computer, display your photos via the computer screen and transmit the photos to family and friends by e-mail. All of these possibilities can add up to an engrossing pastime.

TAKING GREAT PICTURES

The secret of taking a great picture is advance planning and patience before shooting, knowing what you are aiming for, getting each shot into focus and then shooting. Let's look at several types of pictures.

People

If you are planning to take a picture of a group, don't organize them to stand facing you, with smiles on command, like the average Japanese tourist does with a group of grinning compatriots, the leaning tower of Pisa in the background. Withdraw from their midst and take up a position at a discreet distance. Let them relax and get over the pre-photo fussing of making sure hair is in place, compact out to check lipstick and eye shadow in mirror, then hand on hip for posed look.

If you have a zoom lens, all the better, then you can take close-ups of individuals from a distance to record them absorbed in conversation or in any subject other than the camera. Great pictures of people capture emotions as well as faces and dress. Once your subjects are oblivious to your presence, click away, examining each picture on the image window at the back of the digital camera to see if it is worth keeping. If not, you erase; in itself a superb feature of digital photography.

Sports

Sports are all about action, but outstanding pictures of sports capture memorable moments. Try to anticipate these moments when you will get a great picture. For example, a golf tournament, last players are on the 18th green putting out in the final round. Get a good vantage position well in advance, before the players arrive on the green, and then wait for each player's final putt to hit the hole. You have your camera aimed at the player, not the golf shot, to catch his or her ecstatic joy, fist in the air, at holing the putt or the anguish of failure.

Natural views

Say you are taking a picture of a range of mountains with the sun sinking. Clouds are changing shape every few minutes. Get into a comfortable position and, with patience, take your pictures at each change of scene, perhaps a dramatic shaft of light or change of colours.

DOWNLOADING PICTURES FROM
CAMERA TO COMPUTER

As we have seen, the equipment, cable and software, required to transfer pictures from the image recorder in the camera, comes as a standard package when purchasing the camera.

You should also receive an instruction booklet on how to load the software into a PC and download pictures to create files. These files, one for each photo, can be held in the PC either for screen viewing, transmitted via internet to friends or reproduced on paper. The photos can also be transferred from the computer to CD, either for more permanent storage or given to a camera shop for printing if you are not yet ready to do your own thing.

The deletion factor

One of the great advantages of digital photography is the ease of deletion, either immediately after you have taken the shot or later, once downloaded to a PC and reviewed on screen. Care should be taken to avoid over-zealous deletion of what might seem at the time a not-so-good image. A photo may take on a new importance as time goes by and circumstances change. If in doubt, keep it stored on file or CD.

What is compression?

Compression was mentioned earlier and concerns reducing the number of pixels at which your camera is rated. It is a bit technical, but bear with me. It is important to grasp the technique if you are going to process digital photos via a personal computer and transmit via the internet; areas where a lot of the pleasure of digital photography lies.

An image/photo file, taken by a digital camera, is huge in terms of volume, expressed in computer terms as "bytes", compared to normal computer files of text. Therefore, not only does each photo take up a great deal of computer capacity but also transmitting a photo online can take an eternity, especially if your telephone line is not broadband – see chapter 5 Surfing the Web. And you can have a very vexed correspondent at the other end if they have taken literally hours of online telephone time (and expense) to download the file at their end. Have no fear, however, the technical world always has a solution!

Compression is the solution to make computer files more compact and manageable. This is done by reducing the number of pixels of similar colours in any one file that may be surplus to the need for a satisfactory photo.

The degree of compression can be programmed before taking your photos. Digital cameras have a switch providing options for three (high, medium and slight) degrees of compression. With experience, you will find the "happy medium" for a photo that is acceptable quality and results in a computer file which does not exceed, say, 200Kb, which is a manageable volume both for storage and transmittal by internet.

Photos can also be compressed when on file in your computer, using the digital photo software supplied with your camera.

SOFTWARE FOR DIGITAL PHOTOGRAPHY

There is now available on the market a wide range of low-cost software programmes in order to edit for special effects or eliminate unwanted features in the image files stored in your computer. This editing process can lead to learning how to get the composition of a similar shot better next time round.

If you do not have easy access to a store for special effects software, try a search engine like Google or Yahoo and key in "Software Digital Photos". Google will throw up a choice of nineteen million pages of websites for online browsing and shopping! Just goes to show you that this is a highly competitive market. Which means, for you the consumer, choice, quality and low prices.

One leading player in the market of digital photo software is Adobe with its Adobe Photoshop CS website which provides a mass of free online tutorials for the beginners and software packages for custom design retouches to digital photos for embellishment and special effects.

You may also choose to dip your toe in the waters of the wonderful world of digital photos by some advance reading on the subject. Here are a few bestsellers to be found on Amazon online or bookshops:

Digital Photographer's Guide to Photoshop Elements
    by Barry Beckham
How to Make Great Digital Photos
    by Tim Grey
Create and Share Digital Photos
    by P Grupp
Your Lifestyle Guide to Digital Photos
    by J Grall

Now, the grand finale: presenting your photos on screen

There are a number of excellent software programmes available which permit a presentation of photos stored in a PC by way of a screen slideshow on computer (or even a TV set) to a selected audience such as friends and family.

Take the example of a recent experience I had when my wife and I attended a New Year's Eve dinner party, at which some twenty guests were present. On the stroke of midnight, Gérard, our host, proceeded to take snapshots of us all, celebrating the event in time-honoured fashion, laughter, hugs and kisses all round.

Thought no more about it until the following evening when once again we were all together at another friend's house. Gérard arrived in the midst of our chatter with his portable computer tucked under arm and proceeded to set it up on a small table for all to view.

Imagine our surprise and delight when the photos taken the previous evening started to appear on the PC's fifteen inch screen, one by one, the sequence controlled by software giving enough time for viewing. Cries of delight, moans of oh no, is that me, laughter galore, the slideshow was the happening of the evening.

Just one of the many surprises now possible for your friends and family with the advent of a great new pastime.

CHAPTER 9

Stargazing

A BEGINNER'S GUIDE TO THE GALAXY

"Twinkle, twinkle little star,
how I wonder what you are..."

Man the world over has been gazing outwards into space ever since the dawn of humanity to seek meaning and new discoveries in the enigma of the night sky. This chapter will give you a brief sketch of what makes up the universe and some idea of how astronomy can lead to a fascinating and absorbing pastime for the amateur enthusiast.

The Universe, also known as the Cosmos, consists of the multitude of galaxies each of which contain countless numbers of stars, gases and dark matter, literally in digits of a magnitude which defy comprehension.

Speaking of gases, nitrogen and oxygen, our source of life, are in pretty short supply out in space. Hydrogen is by far the most abundant gas, taking up an estimated three-quarters of the universe. Practically all of the remainder is helium, that super-light gas which we earth dwellers use to keep balloons aloft.

The scientific study of the structure of the universe is referred to as Cosmology. On the other hand, Cosmogony, a science within cosmology, is the study of the creation and development of the universe.

HOW THE GALAXY IS STRUCTURED

To start to understand what astronomy is all about, we have first to take a broad look at the Galaxy in which our planet earth is orbiting and learn some of the basic terms used in astronomy.

The *Galaxy*, also known as the *Milky Way*, is estimated to contain 100,000 million stars, give or take a few hundreds of millions, held together by gravity, and may have a diameter of at least 100,000 "light-years" or "l.y.".

A light-year is a unit in astronomy used to define distance in the universe. How often have you heard someone say "Approval for the new project? It's light-years away!" Well, if he or she is really talking about light-years, you can forget the project.

A light-year is the distance in which a ray of light will travel in space in one year, and is estimated to be 9.5 million, million km! (The world of astronomy uses kilometres as opposed to miles). So, all you have to do is multiply the distance of one light-year by 100,000 and, *eh voila*, you have the approximate diameter in kilometres of the galaxy we live in, which adds up to a figure with an awesome number of zeros. And that is only our galaxy, not the universe.

The incredibly vast size of our galaxy is a prime example of the kind of mega-numbers that we are talking about when discussing the cosmos and its elements. The numbers are so literally "astronomical" that they are meaningless, rather like expressing the distance between London and Sydney in millimetres. For such mind-blowing dimensions in the universe, astronomers also use astronomical units (AU). One AU is the average distance between the Sun and the Earth (see below) and is a measure to quantify, in small digits, the vast distances amongst planets and stars and provide a sense of proportion.

Now let's look at the main components of the Milky Way. These are the Sun, which provides light and energy to our planet, and what is called the Solar System.

The *Sun* is a star, about 1 million km wide, and our nearest of all the stars. It has such intense luminosity because it is "only" 150 million km, that is, one AU, away from Earth. This compares to other stars whose distance from our planet Earth is measured in millions of millions of kilometres. That's why they appear as tiny points in the velvety, night sky.

The Sun generates life-giving heat and light to our planet by constant nuclear fusions at its core; a contradiction to popular view that "no nukes are good nukes". It is estimated that the temperature at the Sun's core has to be something like 15 million°C, given its nuclear reactions, with a surface temperature at around 5,500°C, not the kind of place you would want to venture near in a spacecraft. Even this unbelievable temperature is much lower than giant stars such as Sirius, Vega and Rigel where the surface temperatures can go as high as 50,000°C.

The *Solar System* is the name given to the Sun and the nine (possibly now reduced to eight) planets, some of which have moons, that is, rocky or icy satellites, all orbiting the Sun and held is place by massive gravity. Certain planets in the Solar System also have an envelope of gases called atmosphere.

The perennial question that lies behind each space probe to a given planet or its satellites that have an atmosphere is: might this give rise to the possibility of extraterrestrial life? This is precisely what keeps the excitement in man's space mission programmes.

Four of the nine planets, including Earth, are a cluster of "near" neighbours in the galaxy and relatively close to the Sun. These four, in order of proximity from the Sun, are as follows.

Mercury orbits nearest to the Sun and is subject to intense solar radiation that creates fiercely high surface temperatures of up to 350°C and has no atmosphere.

Venus, named after the Roman goddess of beauty and almost identical in shape and mass to the Earth, is the next planet in closest proximity to the Sun, and, after the Sun and Moon, the third brightest object in the sky. Venus has a massive atmosphere mainly of carbon dioxide, which creates a "greenhouse effect" (see chapter 6, Protecting the Planet), resulting in a surface temperature of around a roasting 460°C, which excludes the possibility of the existence of water, the source of any form of life. Like the Moon, Venus goes through a series of phases, which means that it can be seen from Earth in the east in the early morning, known to stargazers as the morning star and the west in the evening, the evening star.

Then we have our planet *Earth*, exactly one AU away from the Sun, which is the sole planet known so far to have human, animal and plant life as we know it, by virtue of live-giving atmosphere, containing roughly four parts nitrogen and one part oxygen, and the substantial oceans, the other unique feature of Earth compared to other planets.

The Earth is reckoned to be about 4,500 million years old.

The Earth spins completely every 24 hours from east to west, which gives us day and night and the international time zones. The Earth, as it spins, also orbits the Sun, each complete orbit taking roughly one year, which gives rises to our four seasons. I say roughly one year because, in fact, the Earth's orbit around the Sun takes 365.25 days that we round off to 365 days for the calendar year. An extra day is therefore added to the end of February every four years to catch up on the slight difference, giving us our leap years.

There are two orbital features of the Earth which stand out; its elliptical (or oval) orbit and the tilt of the Earth, both of which are variable. The Earth's orbit changes from being an almost perfect circle to an oval form. This change takes place every 100,000 years or so. And the Earth's tilt varies between 65.6° and 68.2° over a period of 40,000 years. At present the tilt is increasing. It is these changing orbital features which create an Ice Age which happens to be the norm rather than an exception. At present, we have the good fortune to be in an interglacial period.

Mars, the fourth member of the cluster is known as the Red Planet because of its regions of reddish-coloured dust, often whirled into its ultra-thin atmosphere by wild storms. When the storms abate, the dust lies in dunes. Mars has an atmosphere of carbon dioxide and methane (that inflammable hydrocarbon gas), with an average freezing temperature of –55°C at its equator. Since methane is often associated with bacterial activity, this gives rise to speculation of some form of life. But, again, the methane could be produced from a non-biological origin, such as from its volcano, Olympus Mons, the largest volcano in the solar system and now extinct. It is also reckoned that there has been no life-sustaining water for billions of years. All of which does not paint a very positive picture about life on Mars. We should know a lot more about Mars from the latest NASA probe, the Mars Reconnaissance Monitor (MRO), launched in early 2006 and planned ultimately to orbit the Red Planet at an altitude of 250 kilometres.

Going much further out into space we have what are called the *Gas Giants*, the four largest planets that have thick fog-like atmospheres with no solid surface apparent. They are Jupiter, Saturn, Uranus and Neptune. These planets were visited by the two unmanned NASA spacecraft, Voyager 1 and 2, commencing during the late 1970s and, over the next twenty years, sending back to earth invaluable intelligence on the cosmos.

Both spacecraft are now cruising (in opposite directions, as it happens) in outer space, never to return to planet Earth. Just in case they are found and boarded by aliens from outer space, the two space probes have a special recording on board which provides what NASA calls "sounds of earth".

Now let's look at each of the four Gas Giants.

Jupiter is the largest of all nine planets, being 300 times larger than Earth and orbits the Sun at over 5AU. Despite heat generated by decaying atomic substance, Jupiter has glacial atmospheric conditions and is composed almost entirely of gas, except for a small inner core of rock.

Further out, at 9.5AU, is *Saturn*, the second largest planet and unique in that it has spectacular outer rings which gyrate around it in space to a distance twice its diameter, making it a glorious sight viewed from a powerful telescope from Earth. One of Saturn's moons, called Titan, is particularly intriguing to our space agencies. Titan, first identified way back in the 17th century, was discovered during the 1940s to have a voluminous atmosphere of, well, nitrogen, that life sustaining gas that we have here on Earth and, like Mars, large quantities of methane which, of course, gives rise to much speculation about extraterrestrial life, although, with a surface temperature hovering around –180°C, it would be impossible for organisms, as we know them, to survive.

At the time of writing, an unmanned spacecraft, the Cassini-Huygens, has been in orbit around Saturn and its moon Titan since 2004. And the probe Huygens, launched from Earth riding piggyback on Cassini, has now made a successful touchdown on the surface of Titan.

Currently, the results of analyses of the feedback of data from the Cassini-Huygens mission indicate are that there are, in addition to the existence of hydrogen and methane, similarities between Titan and our planet Earth. This is possibly because they are both of roughly similar size and distance from the Sun. The similarities include features on the terrain arising from high winds, and evidence of infrequent but torrential rainfall and, consequently, rain run-off channels, and volcanic and tectonic activity.

Then we have *Uranus*, which also sports outer rings, and consists entirely of gases, primarily hydrogen and helium and has a slightly greenish look, due to the solar effect on methane gas in its atmosphere.

Finally, there is *Neptune*, the furthest out of the four Gas Giants at 30AU, with a diameter of 49,000 km, and pretty well a look-alike of Uranus, except that it has exceptional winds of around 2,000 km an hour.

The ninth planet of the Solar System has been, up until 2006, tiny *Pluto*, a remote object made up mainly of ice with a diameter of only 2,300 km, by far the smallest of all the planets. Due to its eccentric orbit, Pluto's distance varies between 29AU and 49AU. It is interesting to note that Pluto got its name from a young English schoolgirl when it was discovered in 1930. Mrs Venetia Phair, now aged 87, assures us that she suggested Pluto as the Roman god of the underworld and not Disney's cartoon dog. Her father had contacts in the world of astronomy and relayed her inspired idea to the discoverer, Clyde Tombaugh at the Lowell Observatory in Flagstaff.

Because of its distance of more than five billion kilometres away, little is known about Pluto. Indeed, a NASA engineer recently went as far as to say, "What we know about Pluto could be written on a postcard". To remedy this, in early 2006 NASA launched its New Horizons unmanned spacecraft on a journey to Pluto and its environs; planned arrival in ten years' time. This space probe will swing by Jupiter in a slingshot manoeuvre to use Jupiter's gravitational forces to up its flying speed by something like four kilometres per second or 9,000 mph. All we can hope is that we are around in July 2015 to view the photos radioed back from over five million, million km out in the Galaxy.

In this Pluto mission, New Horizons is flying into what is called the Kuiper Belt, the area of the Galaxy from Neptune and beyond, that is, from 30AU to 1,000AU. The Kuiper Belt contains perhaps tens of thousands of large icy objects which still have to be identified and classified by the International Astronomical Union (IAU), the body charged with naming celestial objects.

In 2003, an orbiting sphere of rocks and ice was discovered and, at the time of writing, was code-named 2003 UB313. This object, estimated to be around 3,000 km in diameter and therefore roughly the same size as Pluto, orbits at a distance 97AU, that is, at a distance of around fourteen billion kilometres from the Sun and may be classed as the tenth planet of the Solar System.

This latest discovery, with the possibility of more sightings of a similar nature to come, thanks to ever advancing telescope technology and probes by spacecraft like New Horizons, has given the IAU cause to have second thoughts about the size of objects that merit the appellation planet. At a meeting in Prague in 2006, the IAU announced that Pluto will no longer be entitled to be ranked as a "planet" but will from now on be demoted to the status of "dwarf planet" along with other celestial objects of similar size and orbiting features. Since only a small minority of the members of the IAU voted on this controversial decision, it could well be amended in the future.

There are also billions of "rogue" objects which hurtle around the galaxy, some of which occasionally threaten impacting Earth. At that point they are referred to as NEOs or near-Earth-objects. These objects are Asteroids, Meteors and Comets.

Asteroids are mini-planets, ranging from tiny in size to objects 10km wide and more, and are composed of rocks. Asteroids orbit mostly in a belt between Jupiter and Mars. Occasionally, Jupiter's gravitational field pulls some objects out of orbit and sends them careering around the solar system becoming, in the process, NEOs. It is known that, over a span of hundreds of millions of years ago, a few asteroids have collided with Earth creating vast craters, such as the one in Woodleigh, Australia and another in Manicouagan, near Quebec.

Meteors are small, bright moving bodies rendered incandescent by the friction of the Earth's atmosphere and are referred to as meteorites whenever they land on our planet. Only as recently as 1908, one such meteorite came down in Tungusta, Siberia with an impact estimated to have been equivalent to a 25 million tonnes of TNT explosion, devastating a wide area.

UFOs, Unidentified Flying Objects, again hit the headlines recently. This time it was through the release of a top secret "for eyes only" British Ministry of Defence report, made public at the request of an assiduous academic from a UK university. The 400-page report, completed in 2000 and kept under wraps for six years, tackles the thorny question of whether little green men out in space might be watching planet Earth from a roving spacecraft. To the great disappointment of all, the answer seems to be "unlikely". More positively, the report indicates that all these sightings by individuals around the world are not a figment of the imagination by demented loners and that UFOs really do exist. They are however not probes from outer space but are more likely to be the result of a visual effect arising from meteors and "magnetic and electrical" phenomena. The report found no evidence of solid matter in UFOs which could cause a collision. Pretty mundane stuff to be classified top secret, don't you think?

Comets, made up of frozen gas, ice and dust and often referred to as "dirty snowballs", lurk in the outer reaches of the solar system, way out beyond Neptune and Pluto in the Kuiper Belt. Fairly regularly, a comet will plunge inwards towards the Sun and, as it melts with solar heat, the ice vaporizes, creating a "tail" of gas, dust and debris trailing behind. This tail can be up to ten million km long! Eventually, the more the comet orbits the Sun, the more the meltdown and they disappear completely. Every five to six years, comets are visible to the naked eye of stargazers.

There has been a recent case of a "rogue" comet going off course. In 1994, the remains of a fractured comet, dubbed by cosmologists Shoemaker-Levy, crashed into Jupiter. This incident sent warning signals to our scientists tracking NEOs.

In 2005, NASA made a major breakthrough in cosmological research using a comet as a testing ground. At a distance of 133 million km out in space, its Deep Impact spacecraft launched what was described as a "washing machine-sized impactor" which collided at a speed of 37,000 per hour with Comet Tempel 1, a fourteen kilometre wide mass of ice, dust and rock, plunged deep into the comet and exploded, creating a crater and throwing up a massive plume of icy debris, all photographed by the latest and most sophisticated technology. Scientists are hoping to gain new information on the original composition of the Solar System at the time of its formation 4.5 billion years ago.

The well known Halley Comet was named after Edmond Halley (1656–1724), the second Astronomer Royal, an honorific title created in 1675 for directors of the Royal Greenwich Observatory. In 1705, Halley published A Synopsis of the Astronomy of Comets in which he noted a comet which had appeared every 76 years between 1531 and 1682 and thus correctly predicted the comet's 1758 visit. According to 11th century Chinese records, the same comet was first sighted in 240BC and has made regular celestial appearances throughout AD. The Halley Comet appears in the Bayeux tapestry since it showed up in that historic year 1066 of Norman conquest fame. Last seen from Earth in 1985–86, the Halley Comet is now not due back on the stargazing scene until 2061.

Then we have the *Stars*, of course, billions and billions of them. How did they get to being what they are, globes of gases, mainly hydrogen and helium, emitting heat and intense luminosity through nuclear fusion? Well, it seems that, since the universe began (see later about the Big Bang theory), changes in temperatures and gravitational forces have triggered the nuclear reactions within clouds of gas and matter, creating stars. Stellar size varies from mini-stars of about 1,400 km in diameter to giants which are hundreds of times larger than our Earth.

Giant stars are highly luminous, either pure white or bluish coloured, medium-sized stars are yellow-orange whilst the mini-stars glow a dull red. Current science of astronomy breaks the stars geography into what are known as Constellations.

Constellations, of which there are 88, are made up of stars forming recognizable patterns in the starry sky. One notable astronomer refers to the "line-of-sight effect" of constellations, that is, joining stars with straight lines to conjure their names.

Astronomers over the ages, most notably the Greeks in centuries BC, have given each constellation a mythical and kind of romantic name, now in both Latin and English.

Thus some well known constellations have names such as Ursa Major, the Great Bear or the Big Dipper; Aquarius, the Water-Bearer; Canis Venatici, the Hunting Dogs; Capricornus, the Sea-Goat; Sagittarius, the Archer; Gemini, the Twins; Taurus, the Bull and Pegasus, the Flying Horse.

On this guided tour of our galaxy, I have left the Moon to the last since it is the only extraterrestrial object on which man has set foot, when, on that memorable day in July 1969, Neil Armstrong and Buzz Aldrin stepped out of the Apollo 11 spacecraft on to the lunar surface. Since the surface of the Moon is a coating of dust and there is no wind or weathering, the traces of the Moon landing are still apparent.

The *Moon*, a satellite of Earth, orbits our planet at an average distance of 380,000 km, which is next door in galaxy distance terms. It is now believed that, since the moon is so near Earth, its origins are from what is termed the Giant Impact. The theory goes that a celestial body the size of the planet Mars collided with the newly born planet Earth and a chunk of our planet floated off to become the Moon.

The crescent Moons, which we see most frequently when moon gazing, are because of "phases" in its orbit around the earth. During its phases, the Moon passes overhead about one hour later each day. It is for this reason that, due to the Moon's gravitational forces on the Earth's oceans, our tides at any given location occur about an hour later each day. Hence, the expression "lunar" tides.

A full Moon, which appears once a month, has dark features which, when compared to the white features, produce the "man in the moon" effect. These dark features are now known to originate from craters caused by the impact of meteorites millions of years ago and, as we shall see later, were first discovered by the Italian astronomer, Galileo Galilei at the end of the 16th century.

The Sun and Moon, as viewed from the earth, can be, at different times of the year, momentarily obscure when an eclipse occurs. This is due to the orbits of the Moon and Earth.

A total eclipse of the Sun, or solar eclipse, occurs when the Moon is in a direct line between the Sun and Earth. At that very point, for only a brief moment, the Sun, as viewed from the Earth, appears as a dark sphere instead of its usual blindingly bright self. As a general rule, four solar eclipses occur annually.

A similar phenomenon takes place when the Moon is blocked from solar light by the Earth's orbit bringing it directly between the Moon and the Sun. At that time, a lunar eclipse occurs and the Moon is a sphere of darkness.

GETTING INTO ASTRONOMY

If you were to decide to examine in greater depth whether astronomy might give you a satisfying way to stay occupied, you could commence by studying its history. Here is an overview of some of the highlights.

The history of astronomy dates back to the last few centuries BC and the beginning of AD when the Greeks were the leading civilisation in the world.

The Greek philosophers, those searchers of truth and knowledge through logic and observation, were the equivalent of today's physicists and scientists. Plato (427–348BC) and Aristotle (384–322BC) were the pioneers of studies of the planetary and stellar structure. Aristotle conceived the notion that the Earth was the fixed centre of the universe, with the stars and planets revolving, as he put it, "divinely", around it. This theory was to prevail through to the Middle Ages.

Aristotle was followed by another remarkable Greek philosopher, Ptolemy who, when living in the great cultural centre of Alexandria in Egypt, then part of the Greek Empire, during the period 127–141AD, identified around 1,000 stars, ranking them according to their brightness, and grouping them in 48 constellations. Ptolemy wrote his renowned Almagest which detailed his discoveries and this became the classic reference for astronomers up until the 16th century.

Nothing much was discovered until the 16th century when Nicolaus Copernicus (1473–1543) made a quantum leap in the state of the art of cosmology. Up till then, the theories of Aristotle and Ptolemy had been accepted without question and had the full support of the Catholic Church.

Copernicus, born in Poland, after studies at the University of Cracow left for Italy where he studied canon law in Bologna and medicine in Padua, developed a keen interest in astronomy. After his studies, he became a canon in the Catholic Church in his native Poland. His passion for astronomy lead him to dismantle Aristotle and Ptolemy's theory of the Earth in a fixed position in the Universe. He proposed the now accepted model of the planetary system whereby the stars and planets, including the Earth, all orbit the Sun.

Galileo Galilei (1564–1642), an Italian astronomer and physicist, was another of the great founding fathers of astronomy. Galileo, with an advanced telescope of own design, was the first to discover the existence of mountains on the moon, the four satellites that orbit Jupiter, the phases of Venus and the rings around Saturn. His support and teaching of the Copernican century-old conclusions that a moving Earth orbited around the Sun, the centre of the universe, was strongly disapproved of by the Vatican as being contrary to the Holy Scriptures. He was ordered to appear before the Roman Inquisition on a charge of "vehement suspicion of heresy". The Inquisition was an ecclesiastical court established in 1232 to seek out and punish heretics and which was notorious for its use of brutal methods to extract confessions. Although Galileo recanted his professional beliefs, the court, apparently in order not to lose face, found him guilty and ruled that he be confined to his villa in Florence where he continued his work on astronomy and physics until his death eight years later in 1642. The late Pope John Paul II finally formally exonerated Galileo in 1992. Suggested reading to know more about Galileo:

Galileo, A Short Introduction by Stillman Drake, formerly Professor of the History of Science at Toronto University and also author of, Galileo: His Scientific Biography.

Sir Isaac Newton (1642–1727), mathematics professor at Cambridge University, was another brilliant contributor to the science of cosmology and, coincidentally, was born the same year as Galileo's death.

One of the breakthroughs for which Newton gained fame was his research into falling objects, notably apples dropping from trees, and in doing so developed his Universal Law of Gravitation. Newton reasoned that if objects were drawn to the earth by gravity, could this gravity not extend to outer space? This reasoning led to the now accepted principle that any two galactic objects, that is, planets, their moons or stars, exert gravitational attraction on each other. An example: the Moon's gravitational forces on the Earth's oceans which create our tides, and cause and control the Moon's orbit around the Earth.

Newton also, amid many other scientific achievements, invented the reflector telescope. By incorporating mirrors into Galileo's refractor design, the Newtonian telescope eliminates colours on the fringes and also provides sharper images. To read more about the life of the man said to have been one of the most important contributors to modern science: Isaac Newton by James Gleick.

Following on the heels of Newton, another notable astronomer, William Frederick Herschel (1738–1822) entered Britain's Astronomy Hall of Fame. Herschel was born in Hanover but took British nationality when he started his professional life in Britain as a talented musician. At the height of his career in music he was organist at the prestigious Octagon Chapel in Bath. When he was 35 years, as a second occupation, Herschel developed an advanced type of reflector telescope and started to study astronomy. In 1781, he shot to celebrity status with the discovery of Uranus, the first newly identified planet in centuries and which is the third largest of all the planets. The city of Bath has a Herschel Museum for those interested to know more.

STUDYING THE ORIGINS OF THE UNIVERSE

To learn more about astronomy you could also read some of the history of Cosmogony, man's endeavours to fathom the origins of the Universe.

It is now more or less accepted that the Universe and its Galaxies came into being with what is popularly known as the Big Bang, an almighty explosion of a hot and dense state creating a fireball of radiation of an ultra-high temperature, even greater than that at the core of the Sun and hot enough for nuclear fusion, which possibly took place about 14 billion years ago. A vast and rapid drop in temperature caused the fireball to expand into space forming what is known as dark matter.

Hundreds of thousands years later, the temperatures fell further and the galaxies were formed from condensation of clouds of gases and radiation, all propelled by gravitational forces. Here is a brief sketch of the historical roots of the Big Bang theory, to this day an ongoing subject of scientific study and debate, with a few of the names of notable astrophysicists who played a role in its development.

George Lemaître, a Belgian Catholic priest, professor of astronomy at Louvain University and a graduate of the prestigious Massachusetts Institute of Technology (MIT), is considered the father of the Big Bang theory. In 1931, Dr Lemaître published a scientific paper setting out the theory that the galaxies were receding at high speed into outer space propelled by what he termed a "primeval atom", a term which never endured. In fact, the expression "Big Bang" was first voiced in 1950 by Fred Hoyle, a leading British astronomer, as a flippant, derisory comment on a scientific theory with which he did not agree!

Around the same time as Lemaître's primeval atom paper, Edwin Hubble, an American astrophysicist, advanced the concept that the galaxies are receding in all directions at speeds in proportion to their distances from the Earth, the further out, the greater the speed of recession. Hubble's work suggested that, in the beginning, the galaxies were huddled together and are now streaking into the back of beyond at astronomical speeds because of a mammoth explosion.

During the 1940s, George Gamow, a larger than life naturalized American born in Odessa, Ukraine, was one of the most fervent supporters of the Big Bang concept. Gamow with his team members Alpher and Hermann came up with the theory of the hot dense beginning of the Universe and the existence of high levels of radiation left over from the Big Bang.

The final pieces of the Big Bang puzzle were put in place in 1964 when two physicists, Arno Penzias and Robert Wilson at Bell Labs, were involved in research by radio to identify and measure source of noise in the atmosphere. They found, by sheer accident, as often happens with quantum leap discoveries, the existence of cosmic radiation, an essential ingredient of the Big Bang theory.

THE "ULTIMATE" SCIENTIFIC EXPERIMENT?

Here is an example of how today's scientists continue to strive to unravel the reactions of the hot dense state that was the origin of the Big Bang. Physicists at CERN, (European Centre for Nuclear Research), a vast experimental facility near Geneva, have built what they call the Large Hadron Collider (LHC), a €2 billion project involving huge machines called particle accelerators, buried 100 metres underground in a tunnel which runs in a 27km circle. In 2007, the plan is to collide two beams of particles, composed of heavy atoms, head-on at almost the speed of light, powered by seven trillion volts and at a temperature of –271°C, colder than the vacuum of outer space, in an attempt to simulate conditions of the Big Bang. The Americans are also conducting similar particle accelerator tests at the Brookhaven Laboratory in Upton, NY with what they call the Relativistic Heavy Ion Collider. Watch your screens for more on these ersatz Big Bangs and cross your fingers that they stay in controllable proportions.

What are the chances of an accident of catastrophic proportions happening during these particle accelerating experiments? Probably in the tens of millions to one against. That said, when you have scientific tests involving elements of the creation of the universe, crashing atoms head-on at near to the speed of light, there are always remote chances of things going horribly wrong. For instance, the splitting of atoms in the collision process could form a "black hole" –see comments later- which would implode and suck in heaven knows what parts of the planet Earth. The weirdest of all possible scenarios would be for a particle accelerating test to explode into a cosmic calamity, involving the entire Galaxy.

These theories are not as a result of me reading too much science fiction but are set out in a book, Our Final Century by Martin Rees, an eminent leader in cosmology and space research and professor at Cambridge University who expresses serious concerns about the particle accelerator experiments at CERN and Brookhaven, tests that are being conducted in the interests of "pure" science only. Put another way, experiments with no benefits expected that would make life better for mankind. Is it all worthwhile, one might conclude? Should we risk the future of humanity merely to satisfy the thirst of a handful of our scientists for greater knowledge and eternal fame?

To have regular updates on these potentially scary research projects, log on to the BBC website, www.bbc.co.uk and key in either "CERN" or "Brookhaven" in the explore space and click on Search.

BEGINNINGS OF THE SOLAR SYSTEM

About 4.5 billion years ago, the Sun was formed by the condensation of a vast cloud of cosmic gases, encircled by a swirling mass of gas, dust and matter. This outer layer of dust and matter eventually solidified and, orbiting by gravitational forces, floated off into space to form the nine planets and their satellites, asteroids, comets and meteors. The Solar System ends at a distance estimated to be about 100AU.

ANOTHER NOTABLE COSMOLOGIST

That remarkable British astrophysicist, Stephen Hawking, also deserves mention in this brief introduction to some of the milestones in astronomy. Some 40 years ago, Hawking was diagnosed to have a neuromuscular disease that gave him a short time to live. Nonetheless, he has since then, despite being confined to a wheelchair and speaking with the aid of a voice synthesizer, been a leader in research in the cosmos, notably into the origin of black holes. In doing so, he has become an international hero of our time.

Stephen Hawking seems to have been destined to play his outstanding role in cosmological discovery because his date of birth in 1942 was, uncannily, exactly 300 years, to the day, from the death of Galileo Galilei, the Italian astronomer. Also, on his appointment to Cambridge University, he took the chair formerly filled by that other renowned physicist, Sir Isaac Newton, born in 1642!

Black holes are massive traps in outer space with a gravitational inwards force (from which no matter or radiation can escape) and lurk in the centre of galaxies, swallowing up passing stars or other objects and thereby increasing their volume. Some are formed when a massive star, or cluster of stars, reaches the end of its thermonuclear life and begins to collapse under the force of its own gravity.

Stephen Hawking's research introduced the theory that what he called primordial black holes were created at the moment of the Big Bang. These were mini-black holes, maybe less than half an inch in size but with a gravitational force of billions of tons, which could suck in other celestial objects and grow proportionally!

In 1982, during a visit to CERN in Geneva to see one of the early particle accelerators, Hawking had a near brush with death through contracting pneumonia, and, when he survived, resolved to write a book for popular reading about the origins and future of the universe. His book, published in 1988, entitled A Brief History of Time, is not only immensely popular but broke records for its duration on the bestseller chart.

STARGAZING

You could also take up stargazing, the title, after all, of this chapter. Observing the night sky, with the constantly changing moon, and constellations, can be done either without visual aid or, better, with a telescope. It is worth noting in this context that someone once estimated that the maximum number of stars, out of the billions in our galaxy, that can be viewed with the naked eye from the earth on a clear night is probably not more than 2,000, but enough to keep one busy stargazing.

There are two types of telescopes for stargazing: either refractor or reflector. The first telescope, developed by the Italian astronomer and physicist, Galileo Galilei was a refractor. Sir Isaac Newton invented the reflector telescope, now referred to as a Newtonian, which gives much clearer and sharper images than the refractor design, by virtue of its use of mirrors.

Stargazing with the naked eye

Those of you who live in cities in northern Europe would be best advised to retreat to the country for stargazing, well away from the polluted skies of the urban areas. A growing source of pollution in our skies, which inhibits ground-based astronomy, is the increased amounts of aircraft exhaust trails, as low cost air travel around Europe surges in volume. That said, some of the best and pleasant stargazing conditions are in rural regions around the Mediterranean.

Stars twinkle brighter when in a position close to the horizon. Higher up, they are less visible because of the rarer atmosphere. Whilst stars are the main elements of a constantly moving universe, they appear to be immobile in the night sky. This is merely because of their being millions of millions of miles away. Distance diminishes movement. Compare a jet plane travelling at the speed of sound, high in the sky, with a seagull gliding overhead and it's the seagull that appears to be moving the faster.

Charting the starry skies

Some stars and constellations can only be seen at certain times of the year because of the Earth being in constant orbit. To find out the changing stargaze scenario at the latitude of the hemisphere where you live, you can consult one of the many published star charts. If you have access to the internet, all you have to do is log on to a search engine such as Google – see chapter 5, Surfing the Web – and key in Monthly Star Charts to obtain a wide selection.

Due to the Earth's constant orbit, most constellations as seen from our planet change position in the night sky. Note however that there are stars which are relatively fixed all the year round. An example: the north pole is marked by a star called Polaris, fairly bright and part of the Ursa Minor, the Little Bear constellation, and can be observed in the northern hemisphere all the year round.

Polaris is easy to locate because obviously it is directly north by the compass. And its altitude at x° above the horizon is, at any location in the northern hemisphere, always equivalent to the observer's latitude of the same x°. So, if you are in, say, the UK on latitude 50°N, you should use this same number to locate Polaris on the northern hemisphere star chart which will cover a 180° view of the night sky (given that the globe has a 360° circumference). It follows that, if observed from the equator on 0°, Polaris is flat on the horizon.

Other constellations such as Ursa Major, or the Great Bear, and Cassiopeia, in the vicinity of Polaris, can also be seen all the year round in the northern hemisphere since they never go below the horizon. These constellations are referred to as being circumpolar.

The brightest superstars

In determining which stars are the brightest, the comparative strength of light accorded to any given star is that which is measured as viewed from earth not per the luminosity at source. It is evident that the further out in space a star is, the greater the dilution of brightness as seen from Earth.

Of all the stars, *Sirius*, also known as *Dog-Star*, in the northern hemisphere constellation, *Canis Major*, the *Great Dog* is the brightest of all, literally the top dog!

A dazzling white, Sirius is reckoned to be 8.6 l.y. (light years) away, has a source luminosity of something like 26 times that of the *Sun* and a surface temperature of about 50,000°C (versus around 5,500°C of the Sun). Indeed the origin of its name comes from the Greek word, "seirios" which, rather appropriately, means "scorching".

In the same league as Sirius, and also in the northern hemisphere, we have *Vega*, in Lyra, the Lyre, a steely blue colour and 25 l.y. away and *Capella*, in Auriga, the Charioteer and *Arcturus*, in Boötes, the Herdsman, an orange-coloured giant, 25 times the Sun's diameter and 37 l.y. out in space.

Alongside Lyra, the constellation Orion has *Rigel*, a mega-star, which, were it not so remote, would be the brightest star of all. Rigel has a source luminosity of a massive 60,000 times that of the Sun. Rigel is 773 l.y. away, that is to say, the light from this star takes 773 years to reach us!

In the southern hemisphere, two giant stars vie Sirius as the top superstars as seen from Earth. These are: *Canopus*, in Carina, the Keel, situated way, way out at 313 l.y. and emitting a blindingly pure white light, more than 10,000 times that of the Sun, is the second brightest star in the galaxy; and *Alpha Centauri* (aka. *Rigil Kent*) of Centaurus, the Centaur, in third place (after Sirius and Canopus) and floats a "scant" 4.4 l.y. away.

Last but not least, the biggest and brightest of them all, but so far out in the galaxy it only makes a bottom place in the top twenty superstars, is *Deneb*, in Cygnus, the Swan, situated in the northern hemisphere lying east of Lyra with its superstar, Vega.

Deneb is a cool 3230 l.y. from earth or 30,000 million, million km away. Put another way, a beam of light from Deneb, arriving on the Earth today, started its journey at the time of the Bronze Age of ancient Greece of the Minoans. Makes you think how insignificant our lives are in the Big Picture of the Universe.

Spotting planets

Even given the immensity of the Galaxy, certain planets
that are our near neighbours can be viewed in the night
sky. Planets have no light of their own, only reflection
from the Sun, just like our planet Earth. Despite this,
Venus and Jupiter are so brilliant that they outshine any
of the stars and Mars can be spotted by its strong red
hue.

To conclude this first look at astronomy, here is a
suggestion. Why don't you plan to spend some time
studying the subject in more detail, the history of
astronomy, and the solar system and constellations?
Some reading suggestions are:

The International Encyclopaedia of Astronomy,
    edited by Patrick Moore
Stargazing,
    also by Patrick Moore
Journeys to the Ends of the Universe
    by C R Kitchin
Big Bang: The Most Important Scientific Discovery
    by Simon Singh
Cosmology – A Very Short Introduction
    by Peter Coles

Also, you should try to view some BBC programmes
of The Sky at Night, presented by Sir Patrick Moore,
Britain's foremost astronomer. This is a series which has
set a record as the longest running show in the history
of BBC television.

Then, plan an autumn break for you and your spouse
in, say, September, when days are becoming shorter but

still pleasantly warm. Select a spot on the Mediterranean coastline, where there are fabulously clear, starry night skies. Before you leave home, get a September star chart for the northern hemisphere.

Once arrived, scout around inland to locate a hilltop giving a panoramic view of the sky. Now you are ready for some real stargazing. With or without a telescope but armed with the star chart and other appropriate comforts, personally I would recommend a chilled bottle of rosé de Provence and two glasses, get yourselves installed on the hilltop after dark. Take a few minutes for your eyes to become adapted to the night sky and have great stargazing with lots and lots of cries of... wow, got it!

CHAPTER 10

Buddy, Can You Spare a Dime?

DOING SOMETHING FOR OTHERS

Charity organizations exist to respond to needs arising from an imperfect world, a world where many human beings are born with physical or mental disabilities, whilst others in later life are struck by disease, terminal illness or disablement by accident or war. Around the world, millions live in abject poverty or in a war-torn environment that takes the lives of parents, leaving orphans without resources. In some countries, many families lack the bare necessities of life: a meal a day and drinking water.

All need help from the more fortunate elements of society and most of us want to contribute in varying degrees. The dilemma is the sheer number of needs, which one has to choose, given our limited resources of time and money.

This chapter is for those of you who are at the stage in life of having the time to devote to some charitable cause. In return, considerable satisfaction can be gained, perhaps by using former professional skills and experience, in doing something positive to help the sick, the underprivileged and downright downtrodden. Such an occupation will, at the same time, provide an opportunity to meet new friends working for the common goal of helping others.

In this chapter, we shall look at:

- how to go about choosing a charity
- some of the ways that charities use to raise funding and how members of the public can assist
- brief profiles of the origins and activities of a small number of charities, both British and multinational
- how volunteers can participate by giving their time.

CHOOSING A CAUSE

Each of us has our own worthy cause, be it the Red Cross, ingrained in our lives for its heroic work tending the victims of war, accidents or natural disasters. Or Oxfam, appearing as it does in all those reports that shock during our daily review of newspapers and television news. Or perhaps the RNIB as we see a blind person, with white stick, tapping their way along a street and, by association, Guide Dogs for the Blind.

There are all those charities who research cures and administer care to people suffering from cancer, loss of mind and memory from Alzheimer, Parkinson's disease, muscular dystrophy, deafness, dyslexia and a host of other debilitating afflictions. The list of benevolent causes is long and can be found through the internet on www. the-british-isles.com, when opened, click on "charities".

Perhaps we are drawn to instances of the need for care by others through personal circumstances or a family member, friend, former colleague or a neighbour in difficult straits.

All charities need funding. Sending donations is an evident solution to help those in need but there are many options open to those who might want to participate as a volunteer to raise funds for charity or help in caring for the disabled and lonely.

FUND RAISING

Since this is an activity where volunteers are most needed, you might want to consider, as you read, how your contacts and past working experience might help to lend assistance to a charity organization.

Here are some typical ways that charities raise the funding necessary to meet the costs of shelter for the homeless, to run clinics and fund medical research and operational expense, including travel to areas of need, afford skilled persons in the field, administration and public relations costs to spread awareness amongst the public.

Donations from the public

Cash collections from members of the public take a multitude of forms, the common principle being ensuring that the public is aware of the collections campaign, followed by volunteers meeting groups of people to request cash contributions.

Here are some examples of what members of the public can do to organize cash collections. Most charities will provide support by way of publicity material, help with local press announcements, whatever it takes to spread knowledge that the collections are being put in place:

- Hold a car boot sale, advertise locally to arouse public interest and ask family and friends, social or sports club members to clear out their wardrobes and attics of all the used clothes, furniture, jewellery, books, and other possessions, which accumulate over the years and lie unused and forgotten. Amazing how the public can snap up these items at bargain prices.
- Arrange a collective meal at a local restaurant with a low fixed-price menu and charge a premium for

attendees, explaining the arrangement to all that the surcharge is in a good cause. And bear in mind that being associated with a charity fund raising is good PR for the restaurant, and also good for business.

- Hold garden parties for groups with drinks and snacks and have a raffle for donated prizes.
- Have a word with local supermarket management and get their go-ahead to have collection cans placed at the check-out counters, with appropriate publicity.

These are only a few of the many ways to raise cash for a good cause. Your chosen charity can provide ideas via its website or local office.

In the case of company employees, companies might accept a matched-funds agreement whereby they would put up an amount, cash for cash, of what the employee can raise by public collection. The agreement can even be featured in the local press and generate PR for the company.

Here now are other ways of how companies, with which you may have contacts, can contribute to charitable causes.

Corporate support

Perhaps your former employer, or a company where a family member or friend is working, would be interested in seeing the positive side of being involved with a charity. Commercial and industrial companies have a vested interest to support charity work. Corporate support for a charitable cause, if properly handled by marketing management, can be good for sales, and can also boost internal staff morale.

For a company, being in partnership with a charity is excellent for its corporate image in the market place, and can also reap benefits for its product brand image as viewed by the consumer. It is fair to say that given equal quality and price, a customer will choose to buy the product from a company associated with a good cause such as the British Heart Foundation or the National Asthma Campaign.

Companies can also contribute to charities through providing free products for sale in a charity's high street shops; or recycling waste such as old computers, mobile phones and printer toner cartridges with the stipulation that the recycle sub-contractor makes a cash contribution to a given charity.

Another way where businesses can lend support to a charity is to encourage employee fund raising. An internal fund raising project can promote team spirit and provide lots of fun outside of the daily grind of business.

Event participation sponsoring

Many charities use sporting and other events to stimulate public awareness of their activities and their need for funds.

Typically, larger charities sponsor a team of volunteers, equipped with T-shirt borne logos, to participate in major events, such as marathons, which take place annually, with full television coverage, in high profile cities around the world. Or they might opt for pop concerts, or abseils – which, in case you are puzzled, are events where young people, sporting the charity logo, descend from a great height the steep face of a building or stadium, suspended on a doubled rope – or white water rafting, a great favourite for thrills and spills. In fact, any event where oodles of spectators are present.

Charities rightly use any event where there is a large public attendance and, of course, a "must" is lots of television crews and cameras, which will beam the participants' charity logos into homes nationwide during the nightly ritual of news hour.

How are funds raised through events like an abseil? Take the example of an abseil down Murrayfield Stadium in Edinburgh organized in aid of Cancer Research. Each participant has to raise a modest sum of money as "sponsorship". For any family member having problems in thinking up ways to raise a sponsorship for such an event, visit www.cancerresearchuk.org.

All of the above event fund raising activities need organization. As a retired person with experience of working with others, you can play a part in making things happen through participation in public and corporate awareness efforts and whatever your personal skills have to offer.

Group treks abroad

Some charities organize group treks through a few of the more fascinating spots worldwide. Here, for example, are some trips, which might be of interest to you, on offer by the Alzheimer Society on their website (www.alzheimers.org.uk):

- trek along the Great Wall of China.
- trekking the Inca trail in Peru. The American-Indian Incas formed a great empire in the 15th century over what is now Ecuador and Peru and many of their splendid palaces, temples and fortifications still survive.
- trek through Rajasthan in India with a visit to the Taj Mahal.
- trekking through a nature reserve in north Vietnam, through remote valleys, hills and forests, and staying in villages hosted by Vietnamese families.
- trek in Iceland in summer (!) through mountains and

permanent ice-caps, with hot springs and geysers along the way.

What do you have to do to participate in one of these adventures?

Pay a reasonably modest up-front fee to cover travel, accommodation and meals, and again raise a sponsorship. This entails raising a specified minimum total of donations before acceptance as a member of the expedition. Alzheimer Society provides lots of suggestions of how to collect the donations. Physical fitness for distance walking is required and if need be Alzheimer will outline a 16-week training programme, in itself never a bad thing. And for baggage on the trek, all you need is a small backpack, the heavy stuff comes courtesy of accompanying porters. A bit like the old days when Henry Stanley, the explorer, followed by his native bearers, emerged from the jungle in Central Africa in 1869 and extended his hand with the immortal greeting, "Dr.Livingstone, I presume?" The charity expeditions also have medical assistance.

Shops

Shops carrying the names of well known charities are now a familiar sight up and down Britain, and provide an important source of funding derived from a community spirit of consumer spending for a good cause. Here are a few notes on how these charity shops source products and how members of the public can back this form of enterprise:

• sourcing products: mostly in the form of public donations of all those worldly possessions which pile up in our homes of today's affluent society, unused for years because either we grow tired of them or, merely, out of sight being out of mind. All these clothes that are out of fashion, or taste, or plain out of our size and shape! Oh, and books that gather dust on shelves because either they are not to our liking or really not worth rereading. Some shops even accept products of the high-tech age like computers, mobile phones and toner cartridges for sale in recycling. In short, drop into one of the shops and get an idea for yourself of the kind of stuff that you could help to find donors or donate yourself.

- support by volunteers: all shops need a helping hand by volunteers on a full or part-time basis. For example, Cancer Research shops welcome volunteers for their sales of books, household and other products, behind-the-counter help, keeping the accounts and drivers for transport.

It may be of interest to some readers to note that giving to charity via shops is less practiced in many others countries in the EU, where there is not the same proliferation of sales outlets bearing the logos of national charities. Could this be yet another intriguing sign of a cultural difference between the people of mainland Europe and Britain?

A LOOK AT SOME OF THE CHARITIES

Let's now take a closer look at two of the best known charities, the Red Cross and Oxfam, another for dog lovers plus a fourth, simply because it tells the story of a woman of humble origins who won two Nobel Prizes and made history by her devotion to learning during the early days of research in the field of radiation and its use to find a cure for cancer.

Let me stress that the charities are chosen merely to give you, the reader, examples of how charities arise and develop over time and how volunteers can participate in either fund raising or benevolent activities My selection does not imply that they would be a better choice for support than many other causes.

The Red Cross

First, probably the best known of all, the Red Cross, or Red Crescent as it is called in Muslim countries, was set up by a Swiss businessman, Henri Dunant shortly after the appalling casualties during the epic Battle of Solferino in 1859. This was a battle involving a total of 270,000 men on both sides, when the French and Piedmontese, under Napoleon III, Emperor of France, drove the Austrians, led by their Emperor, Franz Josef, out of northern Italy. Solferino was the greatest land battle since Austerlitz, 60 years previously in the Napoleonic wars. In a single day, 24 June 1859, 40,000 men were either killed or wounded. Five years later, in 1864, thanks to Dunant, the International Red Cross Society was founded in Geneva.

Around the same time, the Geneva Convention was signed by fourteen nations to mitigate the harm done to military personnel and civilians in time of war and provide a protected status for hospitals, ambulances and care for the wounded.

The British Red Cross was inaugurated in 1870, following the outbreak of war between France and Prussia, a nation formerly centred around the Baltic, now Poland and part of Russia, and which served as take-off point for the new German Empire, created by Chancellor Otto von Bismarck; the start of the nation that 45 years later was pitted, with cannons and poison gas, against the allied forces in the fields of Ypres, Verdun and the Somme, from where comes the Flanders poppy of Remembrance Sunday.

We have much to thank the Red Cross for the lives saved during the unending follies of man's obsession for war. Volunteering to help could be a gratifying experience for many.

To read more about the history of the Red Cross:

Dunant's Dream: War, Switzerland and the History of the Red Cross:
  by Caroline Moorehead

Volunteering
Here is a synopsis of only a few of the ways that anyone, with the time, skills and the will, can assist the Red Cross and, in fact, most of the large charities, quite apart from fund raising already discussed above. Note that the Red Cross provides training courses so that all volunteers are skilled in the tasks required of them and welcomes skilled volunteers to train unskilled volunteers!

- Shops: volunteer participation such as behind the counter to serve customers, sorting and pricing goods donated for sale and shop window design
- Caring in homes: providing company by visits, helping out with shopping and cooking, assisting with mobility and treatment and generally boosting morale
- First aid at events: such as sports, concerts and festivals
- First aid for emergencies: such as road accidents, floods and fires
- Accompanying aid: helping invalids to medical visits and just getting them out and about
- Refugee aid: assisting refugees and asylum seekers,

especially if the volunteer is a linguist.

Note that the British Red Cross does not as a rule send volunteers abroad since its international network has already volunteers of the language and culture in place. On the other hand, national volunteering is easy for people with skills. All you have to do is visit one of the many Red Cross offices around Britain.

To know more about helping the Red Cross, either visit a local office or its website www.redcross.org.uk.

Oxfam

The name Oxfam is derived from a combination of *Ox*ford, home of one of the world's most prestigious universities, and the charity's charter to fight *fam*ine without frontiers. Oxfam is yet another charity whose origins are a result of civilian suffering in wars.

During the Second World War, the allied forces set up blockades to prevent arms and other supplies reaching Greece during the Nazi occupation.

In 1942, Canon T R Milford of the University Church and Gilbert Murray, a former Professor of Greek at Oxford, put together The Oxford Committee for Famine Relief (later to be called Oxfam) with its aims to lobby the British Government to lift the blockade to allow essential food and medicines to reach the people of Greece, and to raise funds to aid other civilian victims of the war across Europe. Its first appeal, "Greek Week", raised cash for the Greek Red Cross.

When the war ended, the charity opened its offices in Oxford with, at street level, a shop for the collection of donations and sale of donated gifts to raise funds to "relieve suffering through the consequences of war". Over the ensuing years, Oxfam expanded by sending teams to provide nutrition, medicines and other supplies to the victims of famine abroad, the war in Korea and refugees still living in camps after World War II in mainland Europe and, in doing so, emerged as a global charity.

More recently, Oxfam has focused on its core activities of helping victims of poverty, conflict and natural disasters, and on the plight of small farmers in developing countries.

Aid in conflicts and natural disasters

In the continuing scenarios of conflicts and natural disasters, Oxfam field directors and teams were despatched to join in the massive international aid efforts in Rwanda, where there was genocide involving around 800,000 people and an exodus of 1.7 million refugees, desperately in need of shelter, food and water. And, more recently, has participated in other humanitarian disasters such as the conflict in ex-Yugoslavia and the tsunami in SE Asia.

Aid to farmers in developing countries

Small farmers in third world countries are unable to compete against the financial and marketing muscle of large food corporations of rich nations, and are faced with unfair pricing competition in world markets because of export subsidies granted to European farmers under the CAP (Common Agricultural Policy).

In parallel with many major supermarkets, Oxfam procures products from the third world at fair prices for sale under the Fair Trade brand in their growing number of own shops. The charity has also created programmes, headed up by on-site Oxfam field directors, to assist third world farmers to improve efficiency, including better techniques for irrigation, planting of crops and rearing livestock. By providing know-how, Oxfam is adhering to that wise dictum of giving poor countries in Africa "fishing rods, not fish".

Oxfam's campaigning in support of the farmers of developing countries revealed that, in 2004, a corporate sugar giant headed the list of EU CAP farm subsidy recipients with grants of over £100 million, much of this in export subsidies, whilst third world producers are limited by quotas in selling sugar into EU countries. Oxfam also revealed that other beneficiaries of EU farm handouts, to the tune of hundreds of thousands of pounds each, included a number of prominent and wealthy British landed gentry. Yes, we do live in an imperfect world skewed in favour of the rich and powerful and we have a lot to thank organizations like Oxfam for standing up for the less fortunate.

To read more about Oxfam and its activities:

Rigged Rules and Double Standards et al (Oxfam Campaign Reports)
    by Kevin Watkins, Penny Fowler
The "Original Bridget" Oxfam Diary
    by Ilene Powell

Fundraising
Oxfam makes use of every conceivable option for volunteers to raise funds for famine relief, be it through events, benefit concerts, parties with raffles, collections and so on. But one easy means to support their activities is either by donating goods to, and/or buying from, their retail operations of 750 shops throughout the UK, comprising second-hand book shops, specialist furniture stores, bridal dress shops, music shops, gift shops and (Fair Trade) food stores. In 2004, Oxfam raised a total

of £17.4 million from its shops to finance humanitarian assistance around the world. The shop operations welcome donations of clothing, books, records, CDs, gifts and furniture for resale. You can even buy online an Oxfam T-shirt and sport the colours for the fight against global famine.

Participating in Oxfam
In the area of shops, there are all sorts of opportunities for volunteers. You can also have your say in cases of extreme poverty at home or abroad since Oxfam is in continual dialogue with British government ministers to generate aid; and in cases of unfair trade to add to Oxfam's agenda with the WTO (World Trade Organization) and the EU. If you are a doctor, lawyer, accountant, teacher or have influential contacts with a large company, you can offer your services to assist in Oxfam's fight against global poverty and injustice. Why not use your education and years of experience to participate in Oxfam's good work in helping the less fortunate? To learn more, visit one of their shops or consult their website www.oxfam.org.uk.

The Guide Dogs for the Blind

Although the idea of using trained dogs to guide the blind is believed to have been conceived as far back as 1780 at *Les Quinze-Vingts*, a hospital for the blind in Paris, it was not until 1916 that a German doctor, Gerhard Stalling put the concept into practice by organizing a school in Oldenburg to train dogs in numbers to assist combatants blinded in the 1914-18 war; a case of a benevolent aid to the infirmed arising from the ashes of war.

The Oldenburg school experiment was followed, during the 1920s, by a highly successful guide dog centre in Potsdam. Potsdam, near Berlin was much later to be famous for the "Big Three" Potsdam Conference when, in 1945, Churchill, Truman and Stalin met for the last time to agree on the ways and means to end the Second World War by defeating Japan.

An American lady, Dorothy Harrison Eustis, who was training dogs for army, police and customs duty in Switzerland, heard about the Potsdam centre and spent several months there studying the methods of adapting dogs for the blind.

Ms Eustis subsequently wrote a piece for the Saturday Evening Post in the US. This came to the notice to a blind man, Morris Frank, who wrote to her saying that he would like to introduce guide dogs to the US. Ms Eustis duly obliged by having Mr Frank come to Switzerland and introducing him to Buddy, an already trained guide dog who was to be the first guide dog in the US. Eustis had, by that time, established a dog training centre of her own in Vevey, Switzerland, which she called *L'Oeil qui Voit* or The Seeing Eye. With the help of a trainer from Vevey, The Guide Dogs for the Blind Association in Britain was established in 1934.

For more on guide dogs, read:

The First Seeing Eye Dogs
   by Burnham Holmes, Judith Clarke
Looking Ahead: Guide Dogs for the Blind
   by Paula Harrington

Volunteering

Guide Dogs for the Blind have lots of fund raising events in which everyone can participate. It also welcomes volunteers who may, under specified conditions, donate a dog to augment supply from internal breeding, labradors or golden retrievers preferred, between ten months and three years old. Or get involved in puppy walking under supervision and with training. Or adopt dogs that may not have made the grade in training or are in retirement after seven years of being a guide dog. There are lots of other ways to volunteer set out in www.guidedogs.org. uk.

Marie Curie Cancer Care

Marie Curie was one of those very special human beings, so special that she, with her husband, lies buried in the Panthéon on the Left Bank in Paris, the former church dedicated to the memory of the illustrious of France. Born in Poland in 1867, of schoolteacher parents, Maria Sklodowska had a quest for learning which took her to study at the Sorbonne in Paris, where she read physics and mathematics. It was there that Maria became Marie when she met Pierre Curie, a scientist, then her husband and partner in research into the curative faculties of radium, a radioactive substance, which they extracted from uranium oxide. In these early days of research of radium, the Curies were unaware of the dangers of radiation to their health. To this day, a century later, their work notebooks are still radioactive.

In 1903, Marie and Pierre Curie were awarded the Nobel Prize for their joint research on radiation.

In 1906, Pierre died in an accident with a horse-drawn wagon on the Pont Neuf in Paris. In 1908, although debilitated by radiation, Marie took over his chair at the Sorbonne University as Professor of Physics, a first for a woman at the Sorbonne. She continued their research and, in 1911, was awarded a second Nobel Prize, this time for chemistry. She also continued her work at the Sorbonne's Radium Institute, which had two laboratories, one to study radium, the other for cancer research. Marie Curie died of leukaemia in 1934. What a remarkable woman.

For more on the life of Marie Curie:

Obsessive Genius: The Inner World of Marie Curie
  by Barbara Goldsmith
Marie Curie (Famous People, Famous Lives)
  by Karen Wallace, Nick Ward

Today, the name Curie remains the core symbol of cancer research in France, with one of the main research centres, *Centre de Recherche de L'Institut Curie*, based in Paris. A museum in memory of Marie Curie forms part of the Pavillon Curie, built in 1914, and located at 11, rue Pierre et Marie Curie, Paris 5, on the Left Bank, not far from the Sorbonne and the Panthéon.

In Britain alone, cancer kills annually 150,000 with another one million sufferers at any given time. The Marie Curie Memorial Foundation was formed in 1952. Now known as Marie Curie Cancer Care, it has nursing centres, called Hospices, located in ten major cities in the UK, providing free care for about 25,000 cancer patients.

The charity also provides outside nursing care to the terminally ill to allow them the dignity of spending what remains of their life at home. Marie Curie Cancer Care has also a centre for cancer research, based in Surrey and a group called Marie Curie Palliative Care Research addressing the issues of people dying from cancer.

Volunteering
Marie Curie Cancer Care relies entirely on public donations to finance its benevolent work. The organization

participates in events, encourages members of the public to fund raise with coffee mornings, bring and buy days, gala dinners, concerts and balls. It also seeks shop volunteers for its 170 charity shops around Britain. In short, Marie Curie Cancer Care uses every means known to charities to fund its good work. For more information, visit their website www.mariecurie.org.uk.

GIVING WHILE LIVING

Now that we have looked at some of the charities and how people with the time and the will can participate to help others, let's look back at how one man, who was at a point in time the wealthiest man in the world, spent his retirement, and his fortune, helping people in need.

Andrew Carnegie (1835–1919) was the stuff that dreams are made of, especially in the late 19th century when extreme poverty in the New World was widespread in the immigrant working class.

How Andrew Carnegie handled his immense wealth is interesting in our modern age when many wealthy persons die, leaving behind them fortunes and all the potential damage that inherited wealth can inflict.

Born in Dunfermline, on the east coast of Scotland, son of a weaver, Carnegie emigrated with his family to the US in 1848 where they settled in Pennsylvania. At the age of thirteen, he started work on the shop floor of a cotton mill, followed by jobs with Western Union and Pennsylvania Railroad. This was the 1850s when industrialisation, rail transport and telegraphic communications in the US were in their infancy.

In 1865, when new immigrants were crowded into urban areas, teeming with crime, filth and poverty, the ambitious Carnegie, now 30 years of age, struck out on his own and founded the Carnegie Steel Company, which launched the steel industry in Pittsburgh.

By all accounts, Carnegie was a brilliant but a hard-hearted and tough employer, as he probably had to be to manage workers and succeed in the hellish working conditions of a 19th century steel mill. Thirty five years later, Carnegie sold out to J P Morgan, the banker, for $480 million, making him the world's richest man at that time.

What has all this to do with charity work? Well, Carnegie's Scottish blood told him that "the man who dies rich, dies in disgrace". In his 1889 essay on wealth, he stated that the rich had a duty to use most of their money to benefit the community, and that they themselves should be active doing just that during their lifetimes.

When Carnegie was a young man, he loved to read. So his logic told him that the sensible thing to do with his money would be to provide free education for those who could not afford it. He proceeded to donate money to towns and cities, starting with his native Dunfermline, to establish public libraries. In all, he donated funds to create over 2,500 public libraries worldwide.

In 1900, he founded the Carnegie Technical College to provide free studies to the young of Pittsburgh's working class. Carnegie Technical, after a merger in the 1960s with the Mellon Institute of Science, became today's prestigious Carnegie Mellon University of Pittsburgh.

World peace was another cause that he supported with his great wealth by establishing the Carnegie Endowment for International Peace, which funded the building of The Peace Palace in The Hague, home of the Permanent Court of Arbitration, popularly known as The Hague Tribunal, which was set up to try to settle matters amongst conflicting nations.

In all, Carnegie gave away about $4 billion in today's money. A keen writer, Carnegie wrote many books including The Gospel of Wealth, where he presented his case that the wealthy should retain only sufficient means for the well being of family and distribute all excess wealth to the less fortunate. He also, amongst many of his writings, produced a biography of his fellow Scot, James Watt (1736–1819) pioneer of the steam engine. Though no saint, Carnegie was, by all accounts, an exceptional man.

To know more about the man, his wealth and philanthropy, read:

Andrew Carnegie
by Joseph Frazier Wall.

Now, here is some breaking news about giving while living. It was announced, in summer 2006, that Bill Gates, currently the world's richest person, is pooling resources with Warren Buffet, the second wealthiest man globally, to devote a sizeable chunk of their immense fortunes to help the many others on our planet sorely in need of assistance.

Bill Gates, who has an already established charitable foundation, is leaving Microsoft to focus his considerable talents on philanthropic activities. Warren Buffet, known as the Sage of Omaha and long time friend and bridge partner of Gates, is donating $37 billion of his net worth to the Gates Foundation. The effect of this pool of vast wealth will permit the Gates Foundation to spend around $3 billion annually, for decades to come, on charitable causes.

The redoubtable challenge facing the Gates Foundation is how best to spend the money. In business, investing in new projects is relatively straightforward. Either you invest in activities where you know the market well and the return on investment is acceptable, measured in dollars or, if not, you scrap the project.

With philanthropy, a foundation is faced by a bewildering multitude of needy causes which have to be sifted through and all angles carefully studied by a diversity of expert advisors. A press report on the Gates/ Buffet tie-up provided a striking illustration of how one charitable venture by the Gates Foundation is leading to another. As a result of a foray into helping victims of HIV/AIDS in India, the Foundation now plans to assist collateral victims of the disease, notably former prostitutes and other poor people, by setting up micro-lending shops to finance small businesses. In this, and all other charitable projects, the benefits accruing from funds spent is virtually impossible to measure with any precision.

This new era of philanthropy stemming from today's business tycoons holds out great hope for the world's sick and impoverished. The likes of Bill Gates, helped by Warren Buffet behind the scenes, with their access to a vast network of brilliant minds in the fields of academics, research science, medicine and multinational companies, should do a thousand times better to help the world's needy than all the self-serving bureaucrats and politicians put together.

To conclude, you might want to give this some thought. If you are a person of means, without deserving descendants, why not plan to embark on the engrossing and satisfying retirement activity in doing something for others with your own estate in an action which is effectively also ultimately a tax saving measure?

CHAPTER 11

Grandma, Tell Us A Story

BUILDING BONDS WITH GRANDCHILDREN THROUGH FAIRY TALES

Most small children love listening to adults reading aloud selections from popular fairy tales but many young parents are often too busy, because of demands from work and family, to have the time to devote to searching for the tales suitable for their children and the telling of them.

On the other hand, retired grandparents have much more leisure time to fulfil this agreeable role of researcher and raconteur for the pleasure of their grandchildren and thus can find themselves engaged in what adds up to an intelligent and absorbing pastime which not only entertains the youngsters but also adds to their growing vocabulary and gives them a gentle guide on moral behaviour as they grow up. Talks with grandparents often remain in the mind during adult life. How many times in your life have you heard from friends the likes of, "my old grandpa always used to say…?"

The purpose of this chapter is therefore to provide some initial ideas to encourage retired persons to study the art of fables and fairy tales and, by learning to change the tone of voice and body gestures like an actor on stage, create enchanted visions, combined with education, in the minds of their young listeners. And, most important, to get to know the children better and form a bond between generations.

In this chapter, we shall also look at some of the best known traditional fairy tales. After each tale, we shall reflect on the moral implications that might be debated with young listeners to hear their views on how these can play a role in their own lives.

There is a caveat to the use of traditional fairy tales to build bridges with growing children. In today's world of a constantly evolving marketplace for all that interests children, be it in the area of toys, books, cartoons, computer games and films ranging from comedy to horror and adventure, all coming on top of their daily delight watching television cartoon programmes, a child's willingness to stick with one subject, especially old fashioned and quality listening like traditional fairy tales, can be relatively short-lived. So, I would suggest that you use the possibly brief opportunity offered by fairy tales to the maximum, enjoy it while you can, and be continually vigilant for a switch to another agenda to maintain the momentum.

ONCE UPON A TIME...

The telling of fables and fairy tales goes back more than two thousand years, that is, to prehistoric times. These tales were spread by word of mouth by parents to children, and thus passed on from generation to generation, until from around the 16th century onwards, when scholars started to put them in writing.

In these tales we meet lovely little girls and boys, fairies, witches, wicked stepmothers, kings and queens, princes and princesses, dragons, giants, ogres, goblins, elves and all kinds of talking animals, bears, wolves, wild boars, sly foxes and young deer, and lots of birds, ducks, swallows, swans and nightingales. There are inanimate objects which are alive, a mirror that talks to pretty girls, a pumpkin that turns into a chariot and a lamp that may have a genie.

All are tales designed to delight small children who, as they listen wide-eyed before falling asleep, have visions of a make-believe world where truth prevails over dishonesty, hard work and diligence are rewarded, and to love and be kind and gracious are the greatest values of all.

First, there was a tortoise and a hare

The most famous of all raconteurs was the legendary Aesop, a Greek who lived around 600BC, when Greece was the world's leading civilization. Aesop's Fables have been loved by countless generations and remain today state-of-the-art stuff. Although no one knows for sure, because there were no records in writing, Aesop is believed to have conjured up some 600 fables; simple tales each with a moral ending. Some of the best known are: The Tortoise and the Hare, moral, you do not have to be the fastest to win a race; The Shepherd's Boy and the Wolf, which gave rise to today's saying "the boy who cried wolf"; and The Wolf and the Lamb which showed that tyrants will use any excuse to do evil. The moral endings are remarkable because they are as relevant today as they were millennia ago.

Here is a specimen of one of Aesop's fables, The Ant and the Grasshopper, which may trigger a nostalgic memory from your childhood. The words used might vary from writer to writer over the centuries, translated from perhaps Greek into another language and then into English. No matter, it is the theme that counts.

In a field one summer day, a Grasshopper was hopping about, chirping and singing to its heart's content. An Ant passed by, bearing along, with great toil, an ear of corn to its nest.

"Why not come and play with me," said the Grasshopper, "instead of toiling in that way?"

"I am helping to lay up food for the winter," said the Ant, "and recommend you do the same."

"Why bother about winter?" said the Grasshopper. "We have plenty of food." But the Ant went on his way and continued its toil. When the winter came, the Grasshopper had no food and found itself dying of hunger, while it saw the ants distributing every day corn and grain from the stores they had collected in the summer. Then the Grasshopper knew: it is best to prepare for the days of need.

Moral

This is a nice, simple lesson for children to learn to think ahead, such as, for example, working well at school to get on in later life. Why not put the issue up for debate amongst your young listeners and see what they come up with by way of planning ahead?

To learn more about fables, with relaxed and enjoyable reading, *Aesop's Fables* is available as a Penguin Popular Classic.

Then, Grandmother, what big teeth you have

The author of some of our most beloved fairy tales was a Frenchman, Charles Perrault, who in 1697, wrote a book entitled Tales of Mother Goose which included such treasures as Sleeping Beauty, Little Red Riding Hood, Puss in Boots and Cinderella. Perrault's tales were adapted from simple folk-tales which over the years had been told by parents to little children sitting in front of a kitchen fire or tucked up in bed in readiness for sleep. With his Tales of Mother Goose, Perrault is considered as one of the outstanding founding fathers of the countless fairy tales told to children over the last four centuries.

Charles Perrault was born in 1628 into an upper class family which gave him a fine education. After taking law exams he became a senior civil servant and in time became a member of the literary establishment in Paris with a seat at the prestigious *Académie Française* in Paris which presides over the French language and culture.

In taking traditional folk-tales and putting them in print, Perrault injected into the text of each many aspects of high society life of 17th century France, with its nobility living in sumptuous castles and manor houses on vast estates, surrounded by courtiers and servants. His tales also appended, in writing, lessons in morality for his child readers.

To remind you of the tale of Little Red Riding Hood, here is an outline of this vintage favourite for children of all ages.

Once upon a time, a very pretty little girl lived with her mother in a country village. Her grandmother, who doted on her, made a red riding hood for her to wear. Henceforth, the little girl was known to all as Little Red Riding Hood.

One day, Little Red Riding Hood's mummy asked her to take a cake to her grandmother who lived on the other side of the wood. So off she trots through the woods carrying the cake. There she meets a wolf who would have eaten her up there and then had it not been for some nearby woodcutters. The wolf therefore engages in polite how-do-you-do conversation and slyly enquires where she is heading. On learning about the grandmother and the cake, the wolf manages to get our innocent Little Red Riding Hood to tell him where her grandma lives.

On parting company, the wolf dashes off to grandma's cottage well ahead of Little Red Riding Hood, who, typical of little girls, meanders slowly by a roundabout route, picking flowers on the way. When the wolf arrives at the grandmother's door, he manages to gain entry by imitating Little Red Riding Hood's voice. Finding the old lady in bed, he gobbles her up and then dons the grandmother's nightclothes, climbs into her bed and sinks beneath the bedclothes with only his nose showing under a nightcap.

When Little Red Riding Hood arrives at the cottage, she calls out to her grandma that she is there and would she open the door. The wolf, imitating her grandma's voice, tells her how to open the door by pulling on a string. As Little Red Riding Hood enters the bedroom, the wolf, under the bedcovers and wearing the grandmother's nightcap, tells her to put the cake down and get into bed to that she can be given a cuddle. Ever innocent, Little Red Riding takes off her clothes and climbs into bed.

Whereupon, she starts to take stock of her "grandma's" appearance. And then commences the unforgettable questions and answers.

> "Grandma, what big arms you have."
> "All the better to hug you with, my dear."
> "What big legs you have."
> "All the better to run with, my child."
> "What big ears you have."
> "All the better to hear you, child."
> "What big eyes you have."
> "All the better to see you, child."

Finally, "What big teeth you have". With his reply, "All the better to eat you up" the wicked wolf promptly gobbles up Little Red Riding Hood.

Moral

This is an excellent tale to teach children to be on the alert to recognize dangerous situations and think up avoiding action. You might discuss situations and areas in your neighbourhood which warrant caution by children.

Since the ending of Perrault's tale is a tad gory for little children, you might want to change the story to make a happy ending, with justice served out to the villain of the piece. Here is how it might go as the wolf invites Little Red Riding Hood to jump into bed for a "cuddle".

As Little Red Riding Hood gazed in wonderment at this strange "grandmother" with such big arms, big legs, big ears, big eyes and, oh, such big teeth, a small cloud, shimmering with sunlight, floated in through the bedroom window and out stepped a dainty little figure, clad in a beautiful white dress and holding a magic wand in her hand.

"I am your fairy godmother," said the little figure, "and I have come to take you back to your mummy. Do not listen to this monster in your grandma's bed, it is not your grandma at all but a big bad wolf and he is trying to eat you up!"

With a swish of the fairy's wand, a golden chariot, drawn by two white horses, appeared and Little Red Riding Hood dived in and closed the door with a bang. Off went the chariot, out of the window and down through the woods at great speed.

As the chariot fled through the woods, Little Red Riding Hood spied a band of huntsmen, armed with guns. She cried out "whoa" to the horses, hauled on the reins, skidded to a stop with turf flying and hurriedly told the huntsmen what had happened. The huntsmen mounted their horses and galloped to grandma's cottage, just in time to see the wolf coming out of the main door, growling with anger at losing Little Red Riding Hood.

With loud cries, the huntsmen levelled their guns and filled the wolf with bullets, killing him stone dead.

Meanwhile Little Red Riding Hood had arrived home and sobbingly fell into her mummy's arms. Never again would she venture into the woods alone and certainly never talk to any wolf that came her way.

Another classic by Perrault is Puss in Boots, or The Master Cat, as it was also called when first published in Paris over 400 years ago. Here is my potted version of the tale.

It all starts with a poor miller dividing his meagre estate amongst his three sons. All he had was his mill plus a donkey and a cat. The eldest son got the mill, the second took the donkey and the youngest inevitably ended up with the cat.

Hungry and without a penny, the youngest son decided that, as an immediate solution to his misery, he would kill the cat, eat the flesh and make a muff with the fur to keep his hands warm. The cat, suspecting this diabolical plan for his demise, suggested that, if his young master would provide him with a bag and a pair of boots, he, the cat, would go off to the woods and hunt for food. Smart thinking, because the son accepted this plan in the hope that it would improve his situation over the longer term. A lesson perhaps for today's politicians to think further ahead than today?

Once equipped with the bag and wearing the boots, the cat put some bait into the bag and went off into the woods. There he managed to entice a little rabbit, not acquainted with the deceit of the world, to put his head into the bag, pulled on the strings closing the bag and killed him without pity. He then swiftly put the second phase of his plan into action.

Bold as brass, off he goes to the castle and asks to speak

to the king. When presented to the king, he says, "Sire, I have brought you a dead rabbit from my noble lord, the Master of Carabas", a title which the cat had cleverly invented. The king was truly pleased with the gift. This ruse was then repeated with a brace of pheasants again earning the king's gratitude.

In his next move, Puss in Boots persuades the so far unwitting miller's son to go bathing in a river where he knows the king will pass with his daughter, naturally a most beautiful princess. As the king and his daughter pass, the cat cries out that his master is drowning. He also cries out that thieves have stolen his master's clothes. The king immediately orders his men to save the young man and provide one of his best suits for the "Lord, Marquis of Carabas", upgrading the initial deceitful title. As all in such tales, the princess falls violently in love with the now impeccably dressed young "Marquis".

As all this is taking place, Puss in Boots has run on ahead and persuaded some peasants mowing a meadow that the fields rightfully belong to the Marquis of Carabis and woe betide them if they do not confirm this if questioned by the king. Sure enough, when the king passes with his entourage, the peasants duly confirm as instructed by the wily cat. The Marquis, who has now cottoned on to the cat's ploy, blithely tells the king that "his" fields always yield a rich harvest.

Puss in Boots, once again further up the road from the king and his entourage, comes upon reapers and, again through dire threats, gets them to promise to confirm, if asked by the king, that the grain they have reaped belongs to the Marquis of Carabis. Sure enough, this comes to pass and the king is impressed by the vast and rich farm lands of the counterfeit Marquis. Last move in the trail of deceit by the cat involves an ogre – one of these man-eating giants that figure regularly in fairy tales – who owns a stately castle. The cat taunts the ogre, simple fellow that he is, into turning himself into a mouse whereupon the cat promptly gobbles him up. When the king arrives, along with his daughter and the Marquis in his coach, gazing lovingly at each other, he decides to visit the stately castle and he is told that it belongs to the Marquis.

Now comfortably ensconced back in his castle, sharing a few glasses of wine with his new friends, the Marquis of Carabas and Puss in Boots, the king is thoroughly convinced he has a wealthy future son-in-law well and truly on the hook and pops the suggestion to him. "Will you marry my daughter, young man?" says the king. The Marquis happily accepts the offer, marries the ravishing princess and, of course, lives happily ever after. Puss in Boots, as instigator of his master's deceitful rise to fame and fortune, also has a life of great luxury. End of story. But is this blissful end of the story one to be told to our grandchildren?

In today's world, the ending of Perrault's tale of Puss in Boots could be a green light to our grandchildren that, to succeed in later life, the best way is with maximum deceit and the least work. Might we not add a few paragraphs to the tale to impress on our grandchildren that crime does not pay?

Supposing, for fun, you were to draft a new ending to the tale of Puss in Boots. Here is an outline of how it might read. An intrepid journalist, surprised at the sudden rise in society of a poor and uneducated son of a lowly miller, decides to make enquiries as to who really owns the "Marquis's" stately castle and fine meadows. He finds out that the properties were once owned by a Lord Ogre, now mysteriously missing without trace after a meeting with Puss in Boots, and his editor splashes his story on the front page with the headline Fake Marquis's Cat Devours Lord Ogre. The police investigate and eventually the false Marquis and his corrupt cat are charged with the murder of Lord Ogre, put on trial in a court of law and end up in prison. Whilst in prison for a couple of years, the miller's son works hard baking bread in the hot kitchens and so does penance for his sins. One night, when in his cell, the Fairy Queen arrives through his window. "Young man, why are you so sad?", asks the Fairy Queen. "I am sad because I miss my beloved wife, the princess, and I long to be with her" replies the miller's son. The Fairy Queen, satisfied that the miller's son has been sufficiently punished for his misdeeds – after all, it was not he who gobbled up Lord Ogre – waves her magic wand and the young man is whisked away on a silver cloud to return to the palace. There the king, with tears in his eyes, forgives his repentant son-in-law and makes him a prince consort. And the princess and her consort live happily ever after. And Puss in Boots? He serves his prison sentence and, on release, spends the rest of his life happily chasing mice in the dungeons of the castle.

Morals

In discussing the moral issues of the Puss in Boots tale with children, obviously you get over the message that dishonest behaviour is unacceptable and is severely punished. On the other hand, the tale demonstrates that, to get on in life, disclosing as little as possible to others until asked, without being downright dishonest, is to one's advantage in climbing the ladder of life. The tale also teaches children that very often, with ingenuity, you can end up very well with what initially seems a very bad deal. And one of the points that Perrault made in his original tale was that being well dressed and presentable plays an important role in winning the heart of a young lady!

To relive many of these fairy tales of your childhood,

you can read:

Fairy Tales
by Charles Perrault, illustrated by Gustave Doré and
published by Dover Publications.

Mirror, mirror on the wall, who is the fairest of them all?
Of all the authors of renowned fairy tales, the Brothers
Grimm are in the foremost in the minds of most people
around the western world. Jacob and Wilhelm Grimm,
born within a year of each other in the 1780s, were
scholars of the German language and, at one point in
their academic careers, professors of German at Göttingen
University.

During the early 1800s, the Brothers Grimm, with Jacob
as prime enthusiast for the project and writer, resolved
to write a collection of the many folk tales told orally
by parents to their children throughout the multiplicity
of small German city-states, and even beyond these
territories. Jacob Grimm therefore travelled far and wide
to listen to people and put their tales in writing, with the
support of Wilhelm who also concentrated on the theme
of the undoubted complexity of German grammar for
his academic writings.

From 1812 onwards, the brothers published several
collections of folkloric fairy tales, many of which had to
be adapted specially for child listeners by eliminating
adult themes. The collections, which also included
tales sourced from a French raconteur, were eventually
published in English in 1823 under the title Grimms'
Fairy Tales. These included well known stories such as
Hansel and Gretel, The Pied Piper of Hamelin, Rapunzel,
The Elves and the Shoemaker, and Snow White. The
collections also contained, no doubt thanks to the French
raconteur, the Brothers Grimm's version of Little Red

Riding Hood, Sleeping Beauty and Cinderella which were originally published by Charles Perrault in France a century previously. Imagine this happening today with the omnipresence of the hordes of copyright lawyers!

The tale of Snow White, also known as Snow White and the Seven Dwarfs, was told in many European countries as well as the German city-states.

Here is a synopsis of the Brothers Grimm's version, probably the most widely known and loved by children because there is a happy ending for Snow White, marrying her prince.

Snow White is a princess whose mother died shortly after giving birth. Her father, the King, remarries a woman who is both beautiful and exceedingly vain. The stepmother Queen has a magic mirror. Often, with head to one side, hand behind the hair, she looks at herself fondly in her magic mirror and murmurs the words which, once heard as a child, remain with us all our lives, "Mirror, mirror on the wall, who is the fairest of them all?" And smirks as she gets the expected answer, "You are, my Lady". However, one day she gets the answer, "Queen, you're the fairest where you are, but Snow White is more beautiful by far."

In a fury, the Queen orders a huntsman to take Snow White into the woods, kill her and bring back her lungs and liver as proof. The huntsman does not have the courage to do such a dastardly act and returns with the innards of a wild boar.

Snow White finds refuge in a tiny cottage belonging to the seven dwarfs. Meanwhile, back in the castle, the Queen consults her magic mirror and, to her anger, gets the reply that Snow White is alive and well and is still the fairest of them all.

The wicked stepmother Queen, bent on murder, tracks down Snow White to the dwarfs' cottage and, after a couple of failed attempts on her life, the Queen, disguised as a peasant woman, manages to get Snow White to swallow a poisoned apple. Believing Snow White to be dead, the dwarfs sadly place her in a glass coffin.

As time goes by, a handsome prince comes along and, seeing Snow White in her glass coffin, falls instantly in love with her. He persuades the dwarfs to allow his men to take the coffin away with them. As the coffin is carried away, it jerks and the piece of poisoned apple is ejected from Snow White's mouth, awaking her from her death sleep. Whereupon the prince declares his undying love for her and proposes marriage.

Not knowing the prince's new betrothed is indeed her stepdaughter, the wicked Queen turns up at the wedding where she is faced with the truth. As a punishment, the Queen is forced to step into red hot iron shoes and dance until she falls down dead. And the prince and his new princess live happily ever after.

Moral
Clearly this tale is a lesson for children to avoid being too vain about their personal appearance and wickedness and jealousy (by the stepmother) will always be found out and punished.

As another example of a folk-tale recorded by the Brothers Grimm, here is an outline of the main elements of *The Elves and the Shoemaker*.

There is a village shoemaker who works hard but, by giving a lot of kindness to others, he and his wife are very poor. One evening they find they have no money for food. The shoemaker decides that, with the little leather he has left, he will make a fine pair of shoes in the hope that a rich man will come along and buy them. He starts to cut the leather but, since it is growing late and he is feeling tired, he decides to go to bed and finish the shoes in the morning.

The following morning, he goes straight to his workbench to complete his work on the shoes and, to his astonishment, he finds them beautifully finished, every stitch perfect. How could that be? Just at that moment, a rich man comes into his shop, sees the shoes, buys them and goes happily on his way. With the money, the shoemaker and his wife buy food and more leather for shoes. The shoemaker again cuts the leather and leaves the pieces overnight for stitching the following morning. And once again, when he gets to his workbench the next day, he finds the shoes beautifully finished.

When the shoemaker puts the new shoes in his shop window, the villagers rush to buy them up, proclaiming how good and warm they are. The shoemaker and his wife are happy because they now have money – but they are curious. Who is working during the night, finishing the shoes? So the shoemaker plans to prepare the leather and leave it overnight at his workbench and he and his wife will hide behind the curtains during the night to see what happens.

Around midnight, from behind the curtains what do they see but two tiny elves – an elf in German mythology was a fairy dwarf – dressed in tattered leaves and acorn caps, getting to work and stitching up the new shoes. Working all night, the elves leave fine shoes ready to be put in the shop window the following morning.

The happy couple, now no longer poor, wonder how they can repay the elves for their kindness and decide that the least they could do is make them some decent clothes to replace the old leaves and acorns that they wear. So both the shoemaker and his wife get to work and make lovely velvet pants, silken coats and tiny boots with silver buckles for the elves. That night, instead of leaving leather on his workbench, the shoemaker lays out the splendid new clothes for the friendly elves and he and his wife hide behind the curtains.

Sure enough, when the two little elves turn up at midnight and see what is neatly laid out on the workbench, with squeals of delight, they tear off their old leaves and acorns and put on the dazzling new clothes. And they are so happy they decide to go off on a long trip, clad in their new finery. Without needing help any more from the elves, the shoemaker makes fine shoes and prospers, and he and his wife, as the saying goes, live happily ever after.

Moral

Easy, this is a nice story for little children of all ages to show them that one good turn deserves another and never to give up hope and there is often a kindly soul who will help when all seems lost.

Try to see the film, *The Wonderful World of the Brothers Grimm*, which came out in 1962 and starred those favourite artists at the time, Laurence Harvey and Claire Bloom. This is a splendid film for all ages, especially tiny children, and includes a delightful presentation of the tale of The Elves and the Shoemaker.

There is also a new Hollywood blockbuster, released in 2005, *The Brothers Grimm*, starring Matt Damon and Heath Ledger as the two brothers, called in the movie, would you believe it, Jake and Will! According to the preview publicity, they are portrayed as con-artists who pretend to protect villagers from spooky creatures but end up with adventures in a haunted forest which shows them to be courageous chaps after all. Well, I suppose that's Hollywood for you...

For reading one of the original works, here is a

suggestion:

Grimm's Fairy Tales
  by Brothers Grimm, Penguin Popular Classics

There was once an ugly duckling

Hans Christian Andersen is another of the best known writers of fairy tales. Unlike Perrault and the Brothers Grimm, who put traditional folk-tales into writing, Andersen was one of the early authors to write fairy tales of his own creation. Born in Denmark in the early 1800s, Andersen was of humble family origins. Indeed, it was only thanks to the King of Denmark (might the boy have been the result of one of the king's extra-marital sexual frolicking?) that, at the expense of the royal family, Andersen was able to go to a grammar school. After a brief career on stage as an actor, Andersen took up writing and had his first novel published in 1835 at the age of 30. The novel was a success in terms of popularity and the same year Andersen went on to have published his book, for which he was to gain international fame, Fairy Tales, followed by two more collections of fairy tales over the next three years. Andersen was a prolific writer and is credited with well over 100 titles. Amongst the best known are The Ugly Duckling, The Emperor's New Clothes, The Little Mermaid and The Princess and The Pea. Nowadays, you may find many of his tales published as illustrated children's books with no mention that the original story was written by Hans Christian Andersen.

Here is an outline of *The Princess and The Pea*, a short story. A young prince is longing to meet the girl of his dreams and marry her but his royal breeding dictates that his future bride must be a princess by birth. So, the young prince travels far and wide to find his dream princess, but to no avail. Any princess he meets is either too tall or too small or just not his type. Above all, how can the royal family be certain that she is a real princess?

Back in his family castle, one evening, during a heavy rainstorm, there is a knock on the door and there, standing outside, is a bedraggled but beautiful girl. Once admitted to the castle and brought before the prince, the lovely girl says that she is a princess. Naturally, the prince is delighted but his mum, the queen, is sceptical. Then follows the point of the story, which is how to prove that she is a real princess.

The queen invites her to sleep in the castle and orders the maids to strip the bed and put a pea under the mattress. And then pile twenty mattresses on top. Not content with this, the queen orders twenty feather covers on top of the twenty mattresses! Now, we shall see if she is a real princess, the queen thinks, primly. The following morning, off the queen goes to the princess's bedroom and asks, innocently, how she slept. Not a wink, comes back the answer, in fact I am black and blue all over. There must be something very hard under my mattress. The very next week, the prince marries the beautiful, now authentic, princess in the finest wedding ever seen.

A simple tale which most of we adults may find a bit ludicrous, not even any ogres or elves or fairies to make it, at least, a fairy tale. But, put yourself in the mindset of small children, seeing the tiny pea under this enormous pile of mattresses, which their grandpa or grandma, the narrator, indicates by using hand gestures and pointing up to the ceiling, and imagine the squeals of laughter which ensue.

Think also of the children being thoroughly amused by the whole idea that princesses are so tender that a tiny pea under twenty mattresses can keep them from sleeping. Therein lies the difference between the delights of childhood innocence and the realism of adult maturity.

Moral

The message to children is that you have to use all your best features to succeed in life, be it your family upbringing or merely just a pretty face! And once you achieve what you were aiming for, be gracious and do not exploit excessively your plus features because people will quickly catch on and you will become unpopular.

Suggested reading:

Fairy Tales

by Hans Christian Andersen and Tiina Nunnally, Penguin Classics

The Princess and The Pea,

illustrated by Robert Ayton, from the collection of Fairy Tale Classics

The I'm late, I'm late White Rabbit

Lewis Carroll was a pen name created by Charles Lutwidge Dodgson for his writings, notably *Alice's Adventures in Wonderland* and its sequel *Through the Looking-Glass and What Alice Found There.*

Dodgson was a tall, slim, rather handsome fellow, with a slight stammer, born in an upper class English family and educated at Rugby School and Oxford during the mid-1800s. He was a brilliant scholar and held the chair of mathematics at Christ Church, Oxford for most of his active life. Amongst his skills outside of maths and writing, Dodgson was talented in the new art of photography, first developed by William Fox Talbot in the 1830s, and specialized in taking pictures of beautiful little girls who star in his tales for children. The Alice of his tales is said to have been inspired from Alice Liddell, the little daughter of his Dean at Christ Church. Alice's Adventures in Wonderland was published in 1865, with illustrations by Sir John Tenniel, and was an immediate success. Alice in Wonderland, as it is commonly known, was followed by Through the Looking-Glass in 1872, making the author wealthy and famous during his lifetime, and now immortal in the annals of children's stories.

Alice's Adventures in Wonderland is a collection of stories which many of us enjoyed during our childhood, giving us memories which remain, albeit vaguely, to this day. Here are a few of the highlights of the beginnings of Alice's enchanted adventures in wonderland.

The tales start off with Alice spotting the White Rabbit, pulling a watch out of his waistcoat pocket and muttering, "Oh, dear! I shall be too late!" and promptly disappearing down a hole. Fascinated that a rabbit could wear a waistcoat and have a watch, Alice, without any more thought, follows him down the hole. Thus begins her Adventures in Wonderland. The hole is very long and vertical and she falls down and down until she finally lands, with a thump, on a pile of leaves.

As she gets on her feet and follows the White Rabbit along a labyrinth of passages, Alice comes to a long, low hall lighted by lamps and with many doors. She manages to open one of the doors and finds that it leads on to a tiny passage not much bigger than a rat-hole. And at the end of this miniscule passage, she can see a beautiful garden. Alice would love to enter the garden but wonders how she can possibly get through such a small passage. That is, before she finds a little bottle with a label which says "drink me". After checking that the bottle is not also labelled "poison", she drinks the contents and suddenly finds herself shrinking to only ten inches in height. Not the least bit concerned by her change in size, even delighted that she is now so tiny that she can get into the garden, Alice goes to the door opening on to the garden but finds it locked. And the key to the door is on a table which Alice cannot reach because she is now so small.

It is at that point that Alice finds a little box with a label which says "eat me" and containing a piece of cake. Of course, when she eats the cake she grows to nine feet tall and her head strikes the ceiling of the passage. Then the White Rabbit re-appears muttering that some Duchess will be cross with him because, as usual, he is late and kept her waiting. Although the White Rabbit disappears again, he leaves behind a white glove...for more, read one of the many original versions of the tale such as:

Alice's Adventures in Wonderland and Through the Looking Glass
by Lewis Carroll, John Tenniel (illustrator) Penguin Classics.

In the sequel, Through the Looking-Glass, and What Alice Found There, Alice continues her adventures of fantasy. These tales are modelled loosely on a game of chess with Alice and the other characters moving like pieces in a chess match. It starts with Alice looking into a mirror and wondering what life is like beyond it. As she passes through the mirror above her drawing room fireplace, she enters a landscape in the form of a giant chessboard. There meets the Red Queen who turns Alice into a white pawn and promises to make her a Queen if she can move to the eighth rank. As Alice travels across the board, she meets memorable characters such as Tweedledum and Tweedledee, the nursery rhyme twins, the Walrus and the Carpenter, the Lion and the Unicorn and Humpty Dumpty who, inevitably, falls off the wall. Through the Looking-Glass is not only great fun reading for small children of all ages but an interesting introduction to the idea of playing chess. Could it be, perhaps, that Bobby Fischer read Through the Looking-Glass when he was a youngster?

Moral
Alice was a plucky child who seized all opportunities for adventure. Be tenacious in your path through life to overcome all obstacles and, above all, always be curious.

TO LEARN MORE ABOUT THE ART
OF FAIRY TALES

If you decide to launch yourself into an in-depth study of this fascinating art of entertaining little children with tales of an enchanted world, you would do well to read some of the work by Jack Zipes who is a Professor of German at the University of Minnesota and is an expert on the subject. Professor Zipes has a PhD from Columbia University and has written many works on fairy tales.

One of Zipes' most impressive works is as editor of *The Oxford Companion to Fairy Tales*, whose 640 pages in paperback contain reflections on the origins of fairy tales and include such tales as Alice in Wonderland, The Beauty and The Beast, The Frog King, Hansel and Gretel, Little Red Riding Hood, The Adventures of Pinocchio, Aladdin, Ali Baba and lots more.

AND LIVE HAPPILY EVER AFTER

Once you are sufficiently immersed in the art, here is a suggestion which could generate lots of fun over quite a long period. Why not put together a composite picture of the enchanted world of fables and fairy tales by gluing lots of little cuttings from magazines, brochures, comics and animated cartoons on a board to make a collage? The collage would contain many of the human beings, real and mythical, animals, birds, insects, objects that talk and, of course, fairies, all of the elements that animate tales for children.

In the centre of our collage we would have a picture of a stately castle, with the king and queen waving regally from one of the windows. Alongside, would be a beautiful princess who has slept for a hundred years, being wakened by a kiss from a handsome prince. Another glued picture would portray a magic mirror who talks to the queen and tells her she is the fairest of them all. In the grounds of the castle, there could be sheep, and a horse grazing, with a tiny boy, the size of a man's thumb, sitting on its head and talking into its ear.

Around the castle, we would have a lake with an ugly duckling, which is really a beautiful swan, a mother goose and elegant long-legged storks. Running across the lawns, you could have a white rabbit, checking his watch.

Then we would have the woods and a little cottage where a widowed mother, with a spinning wheel to make clothes, and her children live, with the grandma living alone in another cottage on the other side of the forest. Oh, and we must not forget a wicked stepmother who resents the rivalry of her beautiful stepdaughter for the love of the father. In the woods we also have huntsmen, with guns held underarm, bent on saving pretty little girls being gobbled up by marauding wolves.

Roaming the woods is a big bad wolf, with its eye constantly on eating up not only the king's sheep but also unsuspecting little girls and boys who talk kindly to him. There might also be Mr Bruin, the bear, Boris, a wild boar, Leo, a ferocious lion and Renard, a wily fox plotting all sorts of mischief. The woods are alive with insects such as nasty gnats that bite, hovering hornets that sting, a queen bee and lots of beautiful butterflies. On the forest floor there is an ant, toiling with an ear of corn on its back, and a frolicking and carefree grasshopper.

Our picture will also include a man-eating giant called an ogre and elves who are mythical, mischievous dwarfs. Finally, our collage of the enchanted world of fables and fairy tales would not be complete without shimmering fairies with magic wands that turn beautiful little girls into frogs, give lonely couples the babies they pine for and conjure up roses during the winter months for a Prince Charming to win the heart of a pretty damsel; and perhaps a winged angel down from heaven to ward off all evil spirits.

What might be the best way of going about putting this collage together? This could be organized as a family project with you, the grandparent, as project director. As director, you could first hold a meeting of all the grandchildren involved and parents, if they want to join in the fun, to decide the framework of the collage and all the elements that should be included. Once the list has been drawn up, tasks would be allocated to each participant according to their age and their familiarity of the kinds of documentation that would yield the cuttings listed.

Here are some suggestions as to sources of cuttings,

apart from comics and animated cartoons. Castles – travel brochures such as for German holiday tours; animals – local zoo brochure, wild life and riding magazines; insects – nature magazines; fairies and angels – fairy tale publications, using a scanner to extract coloured photos and drawings.

Imagine the excitement and challenge for the children, faced with using their imagination and initiative to search for, and track down all of these pictures, and the fun of putting them all together, glued one by one, in an all-family labour of love. And also the joy of children of friends, once the work is finished, standing in front of this collage peering at the pictures and, for the brightest, excitedly discussing the tales depicted.

There may also be great family pride and pleasure if you can find some local art gallery willing to hang the collage for public viewing.

One final thought. Remember what I said earlier about the recall in later life that many grown-ups have about discussions with grandparents when they were little? Using fairy tales to build bonds with grandchildren could be a lovely source for this kind of fond remembrance.

CHAPTER 12

The Art of Being a Cultured Person

INTRODUCTIONS TO PLAYING THE GUITAR, PAINTING, CALLIGRAPHY AND PLAYING GO

When I was casting around for a final chapter, an article on possibly the oldest board game in the world appeared in my weekly news magazine. The article talked about a board game called "Go", which is roughly similar to, but is said to be more subtle than, chess. Go started life in China around 1,000BC and is called "weiqi" in Chinese. What on earth could have weiqi to do with the title of this chapter, "The art of being a cultured person"?

The article to which I refer recounted that the Tang-dynasty in China listed four accomplishments that a person had to have, to be considered cultured:

- plays the lute, a stringed instrument, roughly similar to today's guitar
- be a skilled painter
- be highly rated for their skills in calligraphy, and...
- plays Go.

I thought therefore that it might be of interest if we were to examine each of these leisure occupations for a possibility for retirement with a soupçon of Tang-dynasty style culture.

First, a few words about the Tang Dynasty itself. This was a period in Chinese history, of around three centuries up till around 900AD, during what were the Dark Ages in Europe but apparently very enlightened years in China.

Indeed, the Tang-dynasty is considered by historians to have been a golden age of literature, poetry and art and also of great wealth and territorial expansion. All of which could well qualify the good citizens of the Tang-dynasty as competent judges of cultured persons. Let us then consider each required accomplishment, one by one.

Playing the lute or guitar

The lute is a stringed instrument, similar to a guitar but which is shaped like a pear sliced in two, top to bottom. Its origins date back to 2,000BC in Asia and the Middle East in Mesopotamia (now Iraq). Nearer home, the lute was first played in Greece c.800BC.

Today, the lute is still popular in the Arab world and the word in English originates from its name in Arab, an "Al 'ud". Indeed, the Moors, mentioned in the chapter on chess, introduced the playing of the lute to Europe during their conquest of Spain, which dates the lute's existence in our part of the world at over a thousand years. It follows that the guitar also owes its origins to Spain during the 15th century.

To learn more about the lute and its cousin, the guitar, when on a visit to Paris I visited the rue de Rome in the 8th *arrondissement* which abounds with *luthiers*, sellers of stringed instruments such as violins, cellos, guitars and mandolins...but not many lutes which nowadays are a rare breed, normally requiring sourcing from equally rare specialists who deal in antique lutes. That said, I was able to source some lutes on the eBay website at remarkably low prices, one available from Shanghai.

From a *luthier* in the rue de Rome, I learned that the lute produces somewhat softer tones than the guitar. What about learning to play either instrument?

A beginner to either the lute or guitar does not of necessity require to read music because music scores for the two instruments are available containing both written music, all those black insects clinging to five horizontal lines, and what is termed a "tablature". The tablature indicates, by using numbers, where to place the fingers of both the left and right hands on the instrument to produce each note. With practice, a beginner can achieve the pleasure of a short piece of music within weeks using the tablature as tuition. Playing the lute (or guitar) is easier for the beginner than playing, say, a violin. This is because notes are produced by putting the fingertips alongside "frets" (ridges on the finger-board to guide fingering), whereas the quality of violin notes depends on the movement of a bow by the right wrist and arm while the fingers of the left hand touch the strings without guidance of frets.

Interesting to note that musical instrument strings are made of catgut, a fine strong thread derived from the intestines of, not cats, but sheep or horses. No one appears to know why they are called *cat*gut. Given the lute's antiquity, this is yet another example of the ingenuity of prehistoric man, creating musical sound from animal entrails.

For those of you who are not at all familiar with the lute, visit a music store to get some lute recordings, such as CDs by that consummate artist Julian Bream, best known for his guitar recitals. Compare the lute sound to guitar by listening to Bream's CD of *Spanish Guitar Recital*, with works from the great Spanish composers, Albeniz, Granados and Rodrigo, to his lute playing in the CD, Bream Edition Vol 1 – *Golden Age of English Lute Music*.

Painting for Pleasure

Best results for painting are achieved when you find your niche: what you are good at doing and stick to it. Over time, most artists develop their own painting method applied to favoured subjects, be they landscapes, life, portraits, animals, flowers, you name it; in short, working with what they are happiest and therefore do best. The advent of the digital camera (see chapter 8, Going Digital) may be useful to the beginner painter, who can take shots of the intended subject from all angles, for later and relaxed reference.

The choice of how you express your work has a range of possibilities. Most amateur paintings are what might be termed representational: a picture which provides a realistic view of the subject, embellished by the skill of the artist. This is ideal for the beginner to painting. Still, it is interesting to look at the other styles of expression through painting which depart from realism and stem more from imagination and emotion.

Impressionism emerged first in the second half of the 1800s when talented artists changed tack from the traditional visual realism of paintings, and, especially for outdoor scenes, created a freshness and luminosity through adding light and colour effects to a subject and discarding precise form or shape. The result of this lack of focus on precise lines and shapes, using free, loose brushwork, was to provide an instant impression of the subject as an "unfinished" work of art.

The most famous impressionists were the great French painters of the 19th century such as Monet and his close friend Renoir, Cézanne, Degas, Pissaro and Sisley. The term "impressionist" arose in the world of art when Monet exhibited his great work Impression: Sunrise, in 1875.

There is no reason why a beginner cannot use this approach to painting, even by copying an original impressionist painting. A copy is, after all, an original by the artist who paints it.

Expressionism is further removed from reproducing visual realism, and is where the artist seeks to express emotions, through exaggeration, strong colours and shape distortions. Expressionism had its origins in the late 1800s with paintings by Van Gogh, Gaugin, Toulouse-Lautrec, the Norwegian artist Munch and Russian-born Chagall. Early cubists like Picasso and Braque were also expressionists. The term was also applied to Matisse in the early 1900s who was branded by the art establishment as a *fauve* or wild beast for his emotionally savage paintings.

To read about this remarkable artist's life and works, *Matisse the Master – A Life of Henri Matisse*, in two volumes by Hilary Spurling.

A visit to the Musée du Louvre in Paris will yield a panoply of the works of many of the above artists. Or simply log on to www.louvre.fr to get a first sighting of their paintings and other works. If you are holidaying on the Côte d'Azur, the city of Nice has a museum devoted to the works of Matisse, the Musée Henri Matisse – www.musee-matisse-nice.org.

The German Die Brücke expressionist group was a school of mostly untrained artists, led by Ernst Ludwig Kirchner during the period between 1905 and 1913. The Wallraf-Richartz museum in Cologne has the richest collection of German expressionism. Two contemporary expressionists worth noting are both Scots painters, Polly Harvey and Christopher Wood. Ms Harvey does works on people and architecture whilst Mr Wood paints landscapes which tend to border on abstraction.

View their works on www.pollyharvey.com and www. christopherwood.co.uk.

We have also *abstract expressionism*. This is where realism disappears and is replaced by the canvas covered by paint in a series of emotive gestures as opposed to form or subject. Best examples of abstract expressionists are Willem de Kooning and Jackson Pollock. There is an excellent film, Pollock, which stars the actor Ed Harris as Jackson Pollock, and which features superb scenes of the artist, legs astride and bent over, dipping a stick into cans of paint and slashing dripping paint on to a huge canvas spread out on the floor of his workshop with swift, decisive sweeps of the arm. The end result is abstract, to say the least.

Surrealism is another style of painting (and many other forms of artistic expression such as poetry) which literally involves one's wildest dreams.

The founding father of surrealism was French writer, André Breton who issued a manifesto in 1924 calling on his followers to express in art form what goes on in the unconscious mind.

The aim of the surrealist movement was to liberate people from what its adherents saw as false rationality and restrictive conventions – a sort of green light to a state of intellectual anarchy. The surrealists saw irrational thought, dreams and hallucinations as a natural antidote to the day-to-day drag of real life. In fact, put another way, being a bit crazy and expressing your thoughts in the form of art is a shield from the rigours of the real world.

Salvador Dali, one of the most prominent artists of the surrealist movement and a man of many personal obsessions and fantasies, who was most prolific in painting between 1930 and 1935, summed it up by stating "the only difference between me and a madman is that I am not mad!" The Catalan artist Joan Miro was also a prime instigator of the art of surrealist paintings and other works at the same time as Dali.

If you are in the Costa Brava on holiday, go and see the works of Salvador Dali by visiting his museum in Figueras or at the houses where he lived and worked with his wife Gala, one in Pubol, near La Bisbal and the other in the bay of Portilligat, just north of Cadaques. If you cannot make it to sunny Costa Brava, just log on to www.salvador-dali.org.

Joan Miro's paintings and sculptures are permanently on exhibit in the Fundacio Joan Miro in the beautiful city of Barcelona. Or log on to the foundation's website, www.bcn.fjmiro.es. If you visit Barcelona, you can also view the works of the world famous Catalan architect, Gaudi, his masterpiece, the Sagrada Familia, the Güell park and many other buildings of truly unique design.

What style and subjects to choose?
If you were to follow the example of many retired people and decide to give painting a go as a pastime and are at a loss for ideas, the best starting point is to take a stroll around a district of any city where there are art galleries and go in and look around. At the same time, you could get a feel for the type of paint that you might be happiest with, be it watercolour, gouache, acrylic, oil and so on. Chat with gallery owners and learn.

For a delightful experience, I would recommend that you visit Paris for a tour of the city's many art galleries. The best place to head for is on the Left Bank, and stay at one of the many small hotels just off the Bld Saint Germain, near Odéon, across the Seine from the Musée du Louvre. Now you are in the heart of the art district with splendid streets like the rue de Seine and the rue Jacob, both in the midst of a warren of chic art galleries and antique shops. As an example of how artists specialize, there is an art gallery, just off the rue de Seine, in rue Jacques Callot, a tiny street, complete with a typical, old Parisian bistro on the corner called, appropriately, La Palette. When I last visited, the gallery was exhibiting some of the many works of Zuka, a contemporary American woman artist. Over the last few years, Zuka has chosen to specialize in painting birds, only birds, as a niche theme, which gives her an elegant hallmark in the art world. If you are to take up painting as a hobby, try to find a subject which would give you a similar absorbing interest.

What type of paint to use?
There are a number of basic options from which the beginner should choose. These are watercolour, gouache, acrylic, oil or pastel.

Watercolour paintings are done on special paper, which can be purchased in pads, all sizes, already stretched, with different surfaces and weights and ready to use. Watercolours are the cheapest to get started. All you need is a set of basic colours (there is no white, you use the white of the paper), sold either in tubes or pans, a palette to mix your colours, a brush or two, sketching pencils and, of course, the paper.

Gouache, a painting medium similar to watercolour, but heavier and more opaque, is also used for painting on paper. It is a lot easier to control than watercolour and works well for a sketchy kind of painting where no light effect is desired.

Acrylic paints are very popular and a favourite with beginners because of their versatility. They can be applied equally well to paper or canvas but dry faster than oil. Once dried, they can be over painted without disturbing underlying layers. If you paint indoors, acrylic paints are odourless, unlike oil whose smell can be strong in a confined space.

To begin, there is a wide range of acrylic paints which come in plastic tubes. They can either be used straight from the tubes or thinned with water and used as watercolours. You also need special, bristled brushes, both stiff and soft versions, and to mix colours, you have a choice of palette, either wooden, glass or plastic or, easier, disposable paper palettes. In short, acrylics are a versatile, happy medium between watercolours and oil.

Painting in *oil* is a bit more intricate, if only because of the delay that it takes for the oil to dry, which requires organization of tasks and patience. Oil mixtures come in tubes, are thick and can be diluted by mixing with solvents. Canvas must be treated or "primed" with a special solution and brushes need to be cleaned with white spirit or turpentine. In short, whilst oil is a great medium for painting, a beginner requires tuition or careful study by textbook.

Pastel is another option. Pastel comes as sticks of ground pigment, shaped in drawing sticks. You do not therefore need brushes or a palette since colours are mixed on paper by overlaying or blending. And the special paper, needed for pastel, comes in colours of your choice which can be left exposed for effect.

Learning to paint
Learning to paint is essentially a confidence-building process to overcome the natural mindset of most people, especially as they mature in years, that they lack the

talent necessary to sketch or produce the right colours to paint well. The more you practise, even with doodles, the more you gain that vital confidence.

The market abounds with books on learning to paint. You might well be interested to start by reading a classic entitled *The Materials of the Artist and Their Use in Painting* by Max Doerner. This is a work known in the art world as "Doerner's book", revered by artists and restorers of old masters and first published in 1934. Max Doerner (1870–1939) was Painting Professor at the Academy of Fine Arts in Munich. The sequence of chapters of the book follows the technical development of a painting, with emphasis on the preparation of the materials by the artist. The book is on sale in paperback on Amazon online.

Once you have done some reading or talked with friends who are painters, you could well take some hands-on tuition from a professional. In this respect, there is a very pleasurable way of taking beginner courses in painting. Holidays combined with workshops for beginners!

Either talk to your travel agent or, if you have access to the internet, one website, www.myhouseandgarden.com has links to many sites which offer a week's relaxation with painting courses in such delightful places as Tuscany in Italy, Languedoc and Dordogne in France, Minorca, that sunny island of the Balearics, and in Britain, the Lake District, Devon or up north on the island of Skye. This is easy learning with the fun of meeting new friends taking up the same pastime.

If you want to splash out and really get away from it all with a winter break in the sun, I noted one site which offered a painting course in St Lucia in the Caribbean. There could be worse ways of learning how to be a cultured person.

Here is a final word on the pleasure of painting. Supposing that, after your initiation to the art in some delightful spot away from it all, you return home and proceed to set up your studio in a secluded room with lots of light, perhaps the attic, completely equipped with easel, paper, paints, brushes, palette and sketching pencils. Then get yourself installed, hang a do-not-disturb sign on the door and immerse yourself in the task of melding together shapes, tones and colours to create your very own silent images to the world at large. Could be worse, don't you agree?

Getting into calligraphy

Calligraphy is defined as the art of beautiful handwriting. The word is derived from the Greek "kallos", beauty and "graphe", writing. More precisely, it is the art of producing alphabetic letters of great beauty.

Whilst calligraphy during the Tang-dynasty used Chinese words as a vehicle of expression, the meaning of the words were of no importance since calligraphy is, and remains today, a form of abstract art for any alphabet, be it our own or other world alphabets such as Arabic, Hebrew, Greek, Russian or from Asia. The viewer either finds meaningful pleasure in the shapes of the letters, set in a coloured layout, or is left unmoved. The ancient Egyptian hieroglyphs were also a form of calligraphy.

In their practice of calligraphy, the Chinese use a slim brush whilst Western calligraphy employs a pen with a broad nib.

During the Tang-dynasty, a gentleman called Tu Meng advanced a number of adjectives to describe varying styles of excellence. These included: talented; graceful; mysterious; classic; carefree; exuberant; and, interestingly, *virile*.

Why take up calligraphy?

In practicing calligraphy, creating a unique form for a letter of the alphabet, stroke by stroke, provides a pleasurable and thought-provoking occupation, which is what interesting mind pastimes are all about. The Chinese view the art as a means for people to discover and exercise control over their natural instincts.

It is evident that, since the art of calligraphy involves producing letters of elegant shapes by the stroke of a pen, calligraphy is closely intertwined with the art of the drawing and sketching required in some styles of painting. So, if one were to take up painting, an enhanced capability for expressing shapes through calligraphy is a great plus. The learning curve of calligraphy and lettering includes not just the elegant design of alphabetic letters, but also how to hold the pen, spacing and use of colour to provide an attractive and original background layout.

There are many clubs up and down Britain, such as the National Calligraphy Society, Society of Scribes & Illuminators (SSI) in London, the Glasgow Scribes Club, the East Lancashire Calligraphers Guild or the North London Lettering Association They are all places where you can receive an induction to the art and, once you progress, exhibit your works along with other fellow members. There is also the CLAS in London, which stands for Calligraphy and Lettering Arts Society. The CLAS has a week's summer school, the Festival of Calligraphy, staged at a university campus which switches annually between northern and southern England.

Skills acquired in the art of calligraphy can also be used to produce attractively elegant lettering for scripts such as wedding and other formal invitations, greeting cards, announcements, award certificates, diplomas and even those ornate letters of the opening word of poems and certain prose.

The art is practiced using special calligraphy nibs, fitted to the end of pen holders. This is an advanced model of the kind used during the schooldays of the 1940s, when we used to dip our nibs in Waterman ink every few words, and which were later overtaken by the ballpoint pen, invented by Hungarian-born Ladislas Biro and first produced during the second World War from his exile in Buenos Aires.

To learn about the art of calligraphy, here is some suggested reading:

Step by Step Calligraphy
  by Susan Hufton
The Art of Illuminated Letters
  by Timothy Noad
Beginner's Guide to Calligraphy
  by Mary Noble, a member of the CLAS.

If you can access the internet, you can log on to www. calligraphyonline.org, the SSI website, or CLAS on www. clas.co.uk, both of which give a host of information on the art and how to get involved.

One last observation about calligraphy. Logos, those signs used nowadays in the world of marketing to promote corporate names and brands, are none other than a modern application of the ancient Chinese art of calligraphy.

Which brings us to the grand finale of our search into the talents required to have man's ultimate accolade bestowed on us; when people will say behind our backs, "George? Talented chap, did you know he plays Go?"

Chess is a battle, but Go is war

My most recent sighting of Go in action was in that great

film "A Beautiful Mind" in which actor Russell Crowe plays the part of real-life John Nash, who was awarded a Nobel prize in 1994 in economic science.

The scene is on the campus at Princeton University with a group of students, standing silently watching two of their class, crouched face to face over a board on which small pieces, black and white, are spread. This was not chess, which one might expect on a university campus, but Go. The Chinese have a saying, "Chess is a battle, but Go is war."

A simplified outline of Go

Go is a board game, played using opposing black, 181 in number, and 180 white but similar in shape, equal value pieces called "stones" and a board with a grid of 19x19 lines (or fewer for beginners). In contrast to a chessboard with its 8x8 lines and 64 squares, the Go board contains 361 squares, equivalent to the total number of black and white stones.

For the aesthetically minded, up-market Go sets have white stones that are made of clamshell and the black, of slate. A "must" to store the stones are bowls, normally of wood. During a game, the lids, shaped like saucers, are used to hold captured stones. Oh, and a stone is held squarely on the nail of the forefinger held down by the tip of the middle finger. Not as awkward as it sounds, since the middle finger is the longer of the two, it provides the right balance and the forefinger is supported by the thumb.

When play commences, the board is empty. Like chess, the essence of being a skilled Go player is learning the optimum opening strategies, upon which you can build up a strong positioning of your pieces.

On opening, black leads by placing one stone on the board on an intersection of the lines – rather than the squares as in chess or draughts/checkers – followed by white. Once placed, stones are not moved except when captured by the adversary. A stone is captured when it is encircled by its opponent's four pieces.

Like golf, Go has a handicapping system to level the playing field for the less talented player, who is given a head start with some of their pieces already laid out on the board at the start of the game.

The objective of each player is to establish territorial rights of intersections of the lines on the board similar to an invading army occupying countries. Territories are acquired when one intersection of lines is completely encircled by stones of the same colour.

As the board takes on stones from each player, clashes develop to acquire territories and take away territories from the adversary and capture their stones. That said, Go is not won only by aggressive moves but by a skilful balance of attack and defence, and flexibility in changing game plan.

Due to the multiplicity of moves possible, no two Go games are said to be alike and there are seldom draws. Indeed, the choices of moves in any given game are so complex that no computer manufacturer has yet been able to come up with programmes for an equivalent of Deep Blue of chess fame to challenge the top Go pros.

The end result of each game is calculated by scoring; one point for each territory gained, that is, intersections entirely surrounded by a player's stones, plus one point for each of the stones captured.

One might be tempted to say that Go seems rather like the ideal board game for the campus of a trendy student establishment like the University of St Andrews in Scotland or the lounges of exclusive London clubs where polite silence reigns.

As we shall see later, Go is not just played by ladies and gentlemen of leisure but also by people from all walks of life and professionals who, in Asia, are paid sums equal to those paid to winners of golf and tennis tournaments.

Origins of Go

From its roots in central Asia some 3,000 years ago and played in China since then, Go started to take on a new dimension when, in the 8th century AD it was introduced into Japan, taking the name "Igo" (part of this Japanese name was later adopted in the west as Go). Since that time, Igo has been played by all elements of Japanese society, bolstered by schools set up to promote standards of play and it is now a national passion.

Go in Asia today

Although played fairly extensively around Europe and the US, Go is still a predominantly Asiatic game, vastly popular in China, Japan and especially South Korea where it has a huge public following.

In Japan alone it is estimated that there are about ten million enthusiasts, of which there are around 500 professionals. South Korea, with less than half of Japan's population, has even more players than Japan.

In China, the game lapsed seriously during the Cultural Revolution in the late 1960s when it was regarded as being a pursuit of intellectuals and thus banned. In a more enlightened age, Go is now making a come-back in popularity, with, for example, a fiercely contested annual international tournament between civil servants of China and Japan.

Since international Go tournaments began in 1988, South Korea has racked up 41 wins, versus 10 for Japan and only 3 for China. Thus, South Korea is, for Go, what Russia is on the world chess scene.

Go in the West

The game was only introduced into Europe during the

19th century and then inexplicably took another century to catch on in numbers. It was not until 1958 that a European championship was organized and, about ten years ago, a European Go Centre was opened in Amsterdam. In Europe, there are about a 100,000 who play Go, compared to 25–30 million in Asia.

In the UK, the British Go Association (BGA) is active in encouraging people of all ages to get interested in the game and has its own website www.britgo.org. If you can, surf their website, which will give you lots of information on what the game is about and how to take it up.

One top British player is Matthew Macfadyen, who won the European championship several years running during the 1980s. He has written a book entitled *The Game of Go*. This seems to be the book to learn what the game is all about, although you could also try to get a copy of *Learn to Play Go* by Janice Kim.

Another excellent source of introduction to Go by Mindy McAdams (no relation, at least I don't think so) website www.well.com/user/mmcadams/gointro.html.

To conclude, if, given the pretty high level of intelligence of some of its players, you might feel a little bit intimidated by idea of taking up a game like Go, consider this: in the movie we talked about earlier, A Beautiful Mind, future Nobel prize winner John Nash is challenged on the campus to play Go by an equally brilliant fellow maths student who asks impishly if, he, Nash is afraid to take up the challenge. Nash replies, with a shy grin, "Terrified, mortified, petrified"!

Facing up to a challenge at Go is, after all, a modest price to pay for being esteemed by others to be a cultured person.